ASTRIK L. GABRIEL

THE MEDIAEVAL UNIVERSITIES OF PÉCS AND POZSONY

THE MEDIAEVAL
UNIVERSITIES OF PÉCS
AND POZSONY

COMMEMORATION OF THE
500 TH AND 600 TH ANNIVERSARY
OF THEIR FOUNDATION
1367—1467—1967

by

ASTRIK L. GABRIEL
Correspondant de l'Institut de France

THE MEDIAEVAL INSTITUTE
University of Notre Dame
NOTRE DAME, INDIANA

JOSEF KNECHT · FRANKFURT AM MAIN

Gesamtherstellung: Wiesbadener Graphische Betriebe GmbH

To
STEPHANIE GEHRING

TABLE OF CONTENTS

UNIVERSITAS QUINQUEECCLESIENSIS
THE UNIVERSITY OF PÉCS

The present year 1967* is marked by two important centenaries commemorating the anniversaries of the foundation of two mediaeval universities in Hungary, in the heart of Central Europe. One is that of the University of Pécs[1], a lovely city at the foot of the gentle slopes of Mecsek at the southern edge of the old Roman Pannonia, exposed to the caress of southern winds that once brought the message of the Italian Renaissance to Hungary. Its university was established 600 years ago.

The other centenary commemorates the 500th anniversary of the University of Pozsony[2], a city on the bank of the blue Danube, in the encouraging voisinage of the princely city of Vienna.

An Anjou Foundation

The *Studium generale* of Pécs was called into life 600 years ago by Louis the Great[3] (1342–1382), king of Hungary, scion of the House of Anjou. His father, Charles Robert (1307–1342), of French ancestry, founded the second national dynasty of Hungary[4]. The great merits of the Anjou kings were bringing Hungary closer to the West and making it, as a contemporary said in 1330, queen among the surrounding countries.

9

Louis the Great was one of the last great knights, with his eyes on his ideal, Saint Ladislas, beloved king of all Hungarians, example of chivalry, embodying courage and fortitude, virtues cherished by his people, always exposed to ravaging wars and forceful incursions. The jewel of mediaeval chronicle literature exalting chivalry, the *Illustrated Chronicle* of Kálti Mark[5], was composed in the reign of Louis the Great[6]. Louis was greatly esteemed by his contemporaries. To quote only one, Johannes de Cardailhac, patriarch of Alexandria, papal envoy to Hungary, complimented him saying: "I call God to witness that I never saw a monarch more majestic and more powerful ... or one who desires peace and calm as much as he[7]."

The very nature of the University, when Pécs was founded in 1367, differed considerably from what had been regarded as a university in the original sense of the word in the beginning of the thirteenth century. By now the two archtypes of universities, Bologna and Paris, were almost 150 years old, with the gray hair of three generations on their shoulders.

The newly established universities were no longer spontaneously arising associations. An outside power, be it emperor or king, instituted the foundation, and the pope confirmed it. On the other hand, by the time Pécs was organized, the university as an institution had gained its place between the secular and ecclesiastical power, between the emperor and the pope. While the emperor embodied the universal power and the pope the universal Church, the university took upon itself the task of universal science. Between *regnum* and *sacerdotium*, the university claimed the scepter of *sapientia*[8].

By the end of the fourteenth century, when the University of Pécs was instituted, the influence of the university, without its being fully aware of it, upon secular and ecclesiastical authorities was declining. And there is nothing more dangerous than for someone to act as if he still had power, when actually he has been deprived of it.

By the end of the fourteenth century, the spirit of the first universities was fading away. The origin of the first *studia* sprang from a curiosity that inspired love for search and hunger for wisdom. The later foundations already yielded to practical concessions and professional preparations. They studied rather for *Brotstudium* in the diminishing echo of the enthusiasm of the previous century.

The University of Pécs, reflecting the spirit of the century, was founded by secular power. The fourteenth century, unfortunately, turned its back on the extremely modern ideas of Innocent III (1198–1216) advocating world government. The princes of the fourteenth century listened to and read the pamphlets of Marsilius of Padua (1270–1342) and William of Ockham advocating the authority of the prince[9]. The princes needed well educated men favorable to their political ideas, hence their interest in the educational affairs of their realms.

*Hungarian Theologians in the
Fourteenth Century*

To the middle of the fourteenth century, Hungary lacked sufficiently trained scholars and theologians. In 1345 Louis the Great and his wife, Elizabeth, petitioned

11

the pope to grant the same privileges to Stephanus de Insula, an Augustinian, a lector in Paris, that he would have possessed if he had acquired the doctorate in Paris[10]. In 1353 the same request was addressed by the king to Innocent VI in favor of Nicholaus Nicholai, another Augustinian studying in Paris[11]. One year before the foundation of the University of Pécs, Stephanus de Insula, the only master in Theology in Hungary at the time and already bishop of Nyitra, interceded with Pope Urban V in favor of Petrus de Verebély, also an Augustinian, at the time lector in Paris, requesting his promotion to the *magisterium* in Sacred Theology. The pope granted the petition, ordering that the examination take place in Avignon[12].

Central European Universities

The University of Pécs was the fourth university founded in Central Europe. The first was Prague in 1348, the second Cracow in 1364, and the third Vienna in 1365.

Prague was founded by Charles IV[13], the first emperor since Frederick II to receive some of the admiration paid the Henrys and Ottos of the tenth and eleventh centuries. His original plan in founding the university was not racial; he did not intend it only for Czechs but for the students of the Holy Roman Empire. His desire was almost identical with that of Louis the Great, to strengthen the state of learning in the Empire and prepare men capable of defending the orthodox faith. Though the founder himself was imbued with the spirit of early Italian humanism, the university itself remained tied to the apron strings of scholasticism. German humanism did not blossom fully until the time of Aeneas Sylvius.

The University of Vienna[14] was founded by the sixty-two year-old Duke Rudolf IV in 1365, and, like that of Pécs, did not survive because of the lack of sufficient endowment. It had to be revived in 1384 by Albrecht III, when the University of Paris was torn by the disputes over the Schism. Both universities, Vienna and Pécs, were founded, according to the papal bull, for the propagation of knowledge and truth (*ut veritas propagetur*). But Vienna was more fortunate than Pécs, because its first rector, a German émigré from Paris, Albert of Saxony, the great scientist, had important scholarly connections, while Pécs lacked the leader who could have given even momentary publicity to the new institution.

The University of Cracow was founded by a charter of Casimir III the Great (1333–1370), dated May 12, 1364—in all legal faculties (*in qualibet licita facultate*)—and intended it to be of international character, where students not only from the kingdom of Poland but from other parts of the world (*ex diversis mundi partibus*) would come freely and in security. His model was not the *Studium* of Paris but those of Bologna and Padua[15]. The papal confirmation followed a few months later, on September 1, preceding exactly by one year the foundation of Pécs[16].

But unlike Prague, the three other universities of Central Europe—Vienna, Cracow, and Pécs—were denied a Faculty of Theology[17]. Therefore, the statement of the Hungarian Marxist historian Erik Molnár that the University of Pécs was founded for the training of the Dominicans of Pécs to fight the flagellants and Bogumils is without foundation[18]. How can a school without a Faculty of Theology serve such a purpose, that of training missionaries and fighting heresies? If, as I believe, Hungarian temperament, in general, is ill-fitted for speculative theological studies, it was doubtful that the leaders of the kingdom would have seen the necessity of setting up a theological faculty. Besides, the popes of Avignon wanted the leadership of theological studies to be in the hands of the Parisian masters.

The text of the papal confirmations for all four universities—Prague, Cracow, Vienna, and Pécs—was in general outline identical, edited after a common formula. The purpose of the founding was the promotion of the worship of the divine name, the furthering of the Catholic faith, the increase of justice in both private and public affairs, and the augmenting of the prosperity of humankind[19].

We possess the foundation charters of Casimir the Great for Cracow (May 12, 1364) and of Rudolf IV for Vienna (March 12, 1365) but, unfortunately, the deed of Louis the Great has been lost. The Hungarian foundation, of the same date as Cracow, was preceded by careful preparation and study of the organization of the universities of Padua and Bologna. The royal chancellor of Casimir the Great, Florian Mokrski, was sent to Italy in 1351 to get the necessary information on the organization of the universities. Similar activity was displayed by the emissaries of Louis the Great who, in 1360, requested from Carraro, prince of Padua, the release of Bartolommeo Piacentini (*doctoris legum*) to come to Hungary to teach at the University to be founded there[20].

14

It is not surprising that Louis the Great turned to Italy, noted for its excellent jurists, for recruitment of the first professors for his university in Pécs. The administration of his kingdom, the government of the Church, and royal diplomacy needed trained legists and canonists. A trip to Paris was risky and dangerous and, besides, the training of a theologian was a lengthy procedure. The formation of legists and canonists, on the contrary, was much quicker. The road to the Italian universities was well known to the many Hungarian students who received their legal schooling there in the previous centuries. No wonder that the first professor invited to come to Pécs, Galvano Bettini de Bologna, was an Italian canonist, a *doctor decretorum* of great repute [21].

Why was Pécs selected for the seat of the newly founded university? The answer is threefold: first, political and geographical reasons—Dalmatia belonged to Hungary and the gates of the Hungarian kingdom in the direction of Italy were open and well protected; second, Pécs, the immense diocese of *Quinqueecclesiensis*, was the richest among the Hungarian ecclesiastical bishoprics, well provided to take care of the expenses involved in the founding of the university; third, the consideration that lead the king to select Pécs was the strong intellectual life of the city, with a long tradition of students from the diocese going abroad.

The Hungarian South played a very important role in Italo-Hungarian cultural relations ever since the time of Saint Stephen, who welcomed Saint Gerard from Italy.

15

And let us not forget the Lords of the South were the first political allies of the newly arrived Anjous in Hungary.

Gaude Felix Pannonia

In choosing Pécs, Louis the Great bowed before a long tradition of western ties in Pécs. Its first bishop, the French Bonipert (?–1042), after his arrival in the city, did not lose contact with the humanistic school of Chartres under the direction of Fulbert of Chartres. Through a mutual friend, Hilduinus, he asked Fulbert to send him a copy of Priscian's *Institutionum grammaticarum*, used throughout the Middle Ages as a manual of grammar. In a letter addressed to Bonipert, Fulbert wrote:

> Hilduinus, your faithful son, and ours also, has made known to us the marks of your esteem, and has faithfully reported that you desire one of our Priscians, which I am happy to forward by him. Furthermore we shall most gladly send whatever you ask of us insofar as it is possible, and we shall be very happy to come in person if you need us and so desire, if it be within our power[22].

The Latin tradition of the beautiful city, called Sopiane by the Romans, predestined, its students to seek learning at the Italian universities. Sopiane was already a Christian community in the fourth century, with a Basilica dedicated to the memory of five artists-martyrs beheaded at the order of Diocletian in the vicinity of the city, because they refused to execute a statue in honor of the pagan Asklepios. Carolingian records referred to *Quinque Basilicae*,

16

which, according to some archeologists, meant the Basilica of Five Martyrs (*Ad quinque martyrum Basilicam*)[23].

None of the Hungarian dioceses sent so many students abroad at this period as Pécs and Zagreb, the two southernmost dioceses of the kingdom. The tradition of learning gave preference to the city of Pécs because, of the Central European universities founded in the middle of the fourteenth century, only Pécs was not the seat of a royal residence.

It is no wonder that the papal bull itself underlined the favorable location of the city of Pécs as the most suited from all cities in the kingdom[24] "for increasing the seeds of learning and bringing forth salutary offsprings"[25].

The first Hungarian student known to us at an Italian university appeared in 1208 in Vicenza[26]. The first known Hungarian in Bologna (1263) was Stephen de Bancsa, provost of Pozsony[27]. The first representative of Pécs in Bologna, in 1269, was *Jacobus archidiacanus*[28]. In 1346 Johannes, provost of Pécs, was at an unidentified Italian university[29]. In 1317 a Nicholaus from Hungary was the rector of the University of Bologna, and the year of the foundation of the University of Pécs Johannes de Ungaria from Eger was the rector of the University of Padua. Most favorable intellectual connections were firmly established with Italian cultural centers by the time the University of Pécs was founded.

The bull of foundation was given by Pope Urban V (1362–1370) in Viterbo on September 1, 1367.

"Urban, bishop, servant of the servants of God for lasting memory.

We, although unworthy, have been placed by God's will in the mirror of the highest apostolic dignity. To the degree granted from on high, We direct, as shepherd of the whole flock of the Lord, the keenness of vision given to Us to all the realms of the faithful and their progress and good. Therefore, We gladly grant Our gracious favors and unstintingly bestow the aid of Our timely help to all the faithful in their pursuit of learning, by which the worship of God's name and the Catholic faith is increased, justice is cultivated, public and private affairs are usefully conducted, and the prosperity of all men is augmented.

Thus it was recently brought up in a consistory in Our presence by Our most beloved son in Christ, Louis, illustrious king of Hungary, that he, not only for the good and prosperity of the public weal and inhabitants of his kingdom of Hungary but laudably keeping in mind the good of the surrounding territory, earnestly desires that in the city of Pécs, located in the aforesaid kingdom, as being the most eminent city and most suitable and adaptable for this purpose, there be created and established by the Apostolic See a university provided with every permitted faculty, so that the faith may be spread, the simple instructed, justice preserved, judgment and understanding augmented.

We, considering carefully what has been said above and also the extraordinary purity of faith which both the king himself and his ancestors, the kings of Hungary, and the citizens of the same kingdom have had in the Holy Roman Church, as the king himself and his subjects are known to have it, are drawn by his fervent desire that the kingdom be enhanced by the gift of learning and become fecund with the fertility of letters in order to produce men who are outstanding for maturity of judgment, adorned by the ornaments of virtue, erudite in the teachings of the various faculties, and that there come into being there a fountain of knowledge from whose abundance all men may drink who desire to be engaged in the learning of letters.

We have weighed carefully all these considerations, especially the suitability of the city, which, it is held, would be more advantageous and conducive to spreading the seeds of Christian learning and producing worthy fruit than the other cities of the aforesaid kingdom. Since, too, with fatherly affection I long for the good fortune and prosperity not only of the inhabitants of the kingdom and city but also of the peoples of the surrounding regions, overcome by the entreaties of the said king in this matter, and in accordance with the advice of Our brethren, We have decided and also ordain that there be a university in the aforesaid city of Pécs, that it should forever excel in the faculty of civil and canon law and in any other permitted faculty except theology, that its teachers and students should enjoy and use all the privileges, liberties, and immunities granted to doctors, teachers, and students who are members of a university; that those who have, after a period of time, achieved excellence in the faculty in which they have studied, and seek to have bestowed on them the licence to teach in order to be able to instruct others, and the distinction of the degree of Doctor or Master through an examination by the doctors or doctor and masters or master of the faculty in which the examination will be taken should be presented to the bishop of Pécs or, if the Church of Pécs is without a bishop, to the vicar or official of the beloved sons of the Chapter of that Church.

The bishop or the vicar or official will assemble all the doctors and masters teaching in that faculty. Then he will examine the candidates carefully, either by himself or through someone else, in all that is required for the degree of Doctor or Master, according to the manner and custom which are observed in such matters in the universities. If they are found to be capable and fit, he should grant them the licence and the degree of Doctor or Master.

After passing the examination in the university in the aforementioned city and receiving the licence to teach and the degree that accompanies it, as had been said, they will from that time on, without further examination or approval, have full and free licence to lecture and teach in the aforesaid city and in any other university in which they may wish to lecture and teach, not withstanding any contrary statutes or customs, even though supported by apostolic or other authority.

We wish, furthermore, that the masters or doctors who teach in this university be given a just income by the reigning king of Hungary. Otherwise this letter will have no value or weight.

Let no one violate this Our written constitution, regulation, and will or rashly act contrary to it. If anyone dare to try this, let him know that he will incur the anger of the Almighty God and His blessed apostles Peter and Paul.

Viterbo, 1 September, the fifth year of Our pontificate."

The king of Hungary was notified on September 2 of the same year[30] (Plate no. 1). According to the papal decree, the upkeep of the University and the payment of the professors' salaries were left to the king himself (*ac volumus, quod magistris et doctoribus, qui in huiusmodi legunt studio per regem Ungarie pro tempore existentem in competentibus stipendiis provideatur*). If the king or his successors failed to satisfy this condition of providing the professors with competent stipends, the foundation was to be considered void[31].

Similar to the arrangement made in Cracow, the dignity of the chancellorship, with the granting of degrees in the name of the Holy See, was invested in the local bishop.

The bishop of Pécs who became the first chancellor of the University was William of Bergzabern, a man of great experience in international diplomacy, one of the few foreign prelates at the head of a Hungarian diocese. He was one of the greatest dignitaries in the kingdom: secretary and royal chancellor. The king used his talents in important diplomatic missions: he was sent to Emperor Charles IV to reconcile him with his son-in-law, Rudolf IV, founder of the University of Vienna (William knew the papal court very well.); in 1361 he was dispatched to Avignon, where he must have made a good impression when he offered 3,400 golden florins to the papal court and to the College of Cardinals[32]. On May 23, 1364, Urban V expressed his gratitude in a letter addressed to the bishop[33].

At the imperial court of Charles IV, he met the representatives of early humanism in Central Europe, among them the chancellor of the emperor, Johann von Neumarket (*Noviforensis*), bishop of Olmütz (died 1380).

A bishop with such international relations certainly was influential in convincing the king that the new university should be founded in his episcopal seat. William was not like the bishop of Cracow who tried to sabotage the founding of the university, apparently afraid of the expenses involved[34]. His efforts must have been as important as those of the archbishop of Gnesnen, Jaroslaus Bogoria de Stotniki, for the establishment of the University of Cracow.

William, bishop of Pécs, was not reluctant to support the idea of founding a university and to assume the financial responsibilities because the bishopric of Pécs was the richest in Hungary at the time: in 1361 it was taxed 3,400 golden florins, Cracow and Prague only 3,000.

Unfortunately, the archives of the University of Pécs were destroyed during the Turkish occupation in the early sixteenth century. Concerning the three faculties of Law, Medicine, and Arts founded at Pécs, we have only scant information on the activities of these Faculties.

Privileges

After the establishment of the University the granting of privileges was not long in coming. On September 12, 1367, the pope allowed the masters and students of the new university (*Quinqueecclesiensi studio insistendo*) to enjoy the fruits of their benefices for five years without the obligation of residence at the place where their benefice was located, provided that competent vicars would take care of their respective obligations[35] (Plate no 2).

Pope Gregory XI (1370–1378), in his letter of January 16, 1376, renewed to all the masters and scholars of Pécs[36] the same dispensation from residence[37]. For the execution of his decree, the pope requested the assistance of the bishop of Passau, the abbot of Pécsvárad, and the chancellor of the (Cathedral) Church of Pécs[38].

The University was installed in the interior of the Castle of Pécs, in the vicinity of the present magnificent

23

four-towered Cathedral, which has the romanesque dignity of Mainz and of the Niebelung Stadt in Worms [39].

The First Professor: Galvano Bettini

How can we recall the memory of the first professor, Galvano (Galvanus) Bettini (Bettino) de Bologna, doctor in Canon Law (*Doctor decretorum*), the celebrity at the new university, without remembering what the French philosopher Alain once said: "The dead don't die; it is evident because we are living. The dead think, speak, and act because everything is buried in ourselves" *Les morts ne sont pas morts, c'est assez clair puisque nous vivons. Les morts pensent, parlent et agissent . . . tout cela est en nous.* If there were somewhere a statue of Galvano, the celebrants of the 600th anniversary would have deposited a bouquet of flowers there, not to honor his body but to recall his thoughts *c'est la pensée des morts que l'on veut évoquer et non leur corps* [40].

Galvano was a native of Bologna, raised in Padua, who became master of Canon Law in the same university. In 1371 he was already in Pécs teaching Canon Law. A Harvard professor of today could envy his salary which amounted to 300 silver marks, or 600 golden florins. In addition, he received the tithes of the village of Ürög, a charming settlement (*falú*) on the outskirts of Pécs, revenues totaling 70 marks. As a bonus, we might say, he was given a house in the heart of the city [41].

The Italian law professor at Pécs was definitely more fortunate than his Polish colleagues in Cracow, where a Professor of Canon Law (*Doctor decretorum*) earned only

40 marks, one-eighth of what Galvano received in Hungary[42]. Mediaeval astrologists ranged Hungary among the Sagittarians, and according to them, the *Sagittarius* is a generous man by nature.

Louis the Great used Galvano's knowledge on diplomatic missions. On September 27, 1372, the law professor of Pécs and Albert of Waschenstein, canon of Pécs, were sent in embassy to Gregory XI[43].

Unfortunately, Galvano's career at Pécs did not last long; apparently after the death of his generous chancellor, William, he returned to his native Bologna. However, spoiled by Hungary, even in Bologna he remained sensitive to good revenues. Not content with what he was paid, he requested a special salary from the pope, who, on August 3, 1374, from Ville-Neuve near Avignon, raised his salary from 60 to 240 golden florins, giving as a reason Galvano's praiseworthy work in Pécs and Padua[44] (Plate no. 3). From 1379 to 1382 he was again at Padua, but in 1383 he went back to Bologna, with a special request in his travelling bag for 200 golden florins of revenue and, for three years, an additional 100 florins because his two sons were studying in Bologna.

Among his works, *De differentiis Legum et Causarum*, a comparison between Roman and ecclesiastical laws, was printed several times, first together with the *Summa Goffredi* at Venice in 1491[45]. One of his interesting treatises, *Repetitio in Glossa. Opinionem Cap. I De constitutione*, in which Galvano showed himself defensor of the opinions of Joannes Andrea (1270–1348), a canonist called "source and trumpet of Law" (*fons et tuba juris*), was written during his stay at the University of Pécs in 1371[46].

We have some indirect information of another professor who may have taught at the University of Pécs. We learn from the *Liber decanorum* of the University of Prague that in 1379 Master Hermannus Lurcz, originally from Nürnberg, was received into the corporation from the University of Pécs. It is possible that he had obtained his master of Arts degree at Pécs, or perhaps was invited from another univeristy, as already master, to teach in Pécs[47].

At Prague several German bachelors studied under him at the Faculty of Arts. We know of Nicholas Heylprunn and Johannes Kostnic (March 4, 1380) and Frederick Rabenolt (March 6 of the same year), who made their *determinatio* under him[48]. The last trace of his stay in Prague was his functionning at the *determinatio* of Johannes Zaran from Breslau on March 18, 1382[49].

A very agile and active master, from Prague he went to Vienna, where he was registered *intitulatus* in April 1386 at the University, his title given as Doctor in Medicine. On April 13, 1387, he was elected rector of the University of Vienna, referred to as "Master of Arts, Doctor in Medicine and Bachelor in Theology, Rector of Holfeld in Bamberg"[50].

He was the first rector elected from the Faculty of Medicine. He was fortunate to be in Vienna in the years when the great theologian, a refugee from Paris, Henry of Langenstein, was teaching at the University[51]. Most probably he went to Vienna at the invitation of Albrecht III to serve on the faculty of the newly established university.

Curiously, no works of medical nature written by Hermannus survived, only a theological work is known: *Tractatus de Paralogismis et argutiis sophisticis consuetis fieri circa materiam individuae et beatissimae Trinitatis*[52].

Among the doctors of Pécs was Paul, provost of Szeben (*prepositus Cibiniensis*). On April 2, 1369, Pope Urban V ordered Cato, provost of Bács in Hungary, to confer the dignity of doctor in Canon Law upon Paul, observing the privileges, statutes, and customs of the University of Pécs[53] (Plate no. 4).

Wandering Students

Mediaeval students frequented several universities. In Prague, besides Hermannus Lurcz, former Master at the University of Pécs, we know of another student at the University, Petrus de Wydera, *baccalarius Quinqueecclesiarum*, who was incorporated in 1384 as bachelor of Arts from Pécs and apparently received his baccalaureate in Prague in 1396 under Master Joannes Artsen from the Bavarian Nation[54].

On the impulse of the uprise of studies at Pécs, we find several subjects of the diocese of Pécs at Prague in the years following the foundation. Stephen of Pécs was there in 1375[55]; Andrew of Pécs together with Stephen from Szerém obtained the degree of Bachelor of Arts from there in 1385[56].

There is an old proverb: the good scholar never makes history. Though we do not know the roster of industrious students at the old University of Pécs, the names of a few troublemakers or victims of calamities have survived. The students of Pécs were not any better than the irascible *galoches* of mediaeval Paris, the pugnacious companions of Villon, or the quarrelsome students of Bologna. Neither was the Hungarian temperament an easy thing for the rectors and schoolmasters at the University of Pécs to control.

Thanks to several petitions addressed to the Roman Court asking for dispensation from homicide committed when the petitioners were young, we learn the names of a few students who studied at Pécs. They were all involved, in one way or another, in fierce fighting around their schoolyard. This schoolyard battle has preserved for us the very Hungarian-sounding names of three or four students.

Around 1400–1402 we encounter in papal records four real Hungarian names: Csót-Benedek-fia György [Georgius Csót Benedekson], Szöllősi-Fábian-fia György [Georgius Szöllősi-Fabianson], Kanczellár János [Johannes Kanczellár], and László-fia Lukács [Lucas Ladislasson].

The first such incident erupted from the antagonism of Georgius Csót Benedekson, a clerk from Zagreb, and Johannes Kanczellár, a student from Pécs. According to the account sent to Rome by Georgius from Zagreb, on one occasion he saw Johannes from Pécs approaching him, armed to the teeth, carrying a good supply of weapons, arrows, bow, and sword (*armatus arcu, gladio sagittis*). Another bystander, a fellow student, Georgius Szöllősi-Fabianson, suspecting a fight, ran for help, calling upon the headmaster of the school. The latter immediately interrupted his lecture and ran to separate the two hostile scholars, trying to do justice among them. In the heat of the discussion—the fellow from Zagreb still telling the story—the pupil from Pécs hit the master with a stick (*cum quodam baculo ad caput verberare conabatur*). The unfortunate rector started to cry for help, and at this moment the fellow from Zagreb, not very gallantly, shot the student from Pécs, Johannes Kanczellár, from behind, with an arrow in the eyes. (He died three days later.) That everything did not happen as had been reported to Rome and that the story was one sidedly recounted appears from the deposition of the third student, Georgius Szöllősi-Fabianson. One wonders if the student from Pécs, as the fellow from Zagreb so accused him, was really armed with bow, arrows, and sword. (We may ask how he was able with two hands to also carry a stick.) Most important for us is that, whether foes or friends, they all resided in Pécs, "in search of the pearl of science", as the rescript said: *causa acquirendi scientie margaritam*[57].

Another such incident was reported by László-fia Lukács [Lucas Ladislasson], also a cleric from Pécs. He was playing with a knife in the presence of another student, identified only as "Acolytus", who was amusing himself with no less a toy than a whip. According to Lucas, he "accidentally" and not with evil intent, hit the arm of the other student, who, because of later complications and inadequate medical attention, died fom infection of the wounds. Before his death he declared that his wounds were accidentally caused [58].

These records clearly show that the Hungarian students from Pécs matched their Parisian counterparts. No university regulations could have stopped them from carrying dangerous arms.

Just two years before the founding of the University of Pécs, students from Paris in 1365, armed with swords, sticks, and stones, attacked, in the heart of the city at the present Place Maubert, the sergeants of the king who were returning from a mission "politely and in peace". In the heat of the battle a student was killed on the premises [59].

Chancellor Alsányi

Bishop William was succeeded in his seat by Valentin Alsányi (Alsányi Bálint, 1374–1408), a less generous chancellor than his predecessor. At the beginning of 1376, he complained that his possessions and revenues were occupied by religious and secular authorities, dukes, counts, barons, soldiers, nobles, and laymen [60].

The new chancellor belonged to one of the most distinguished Hungarian families; his mother was Ilona Gara, who brought the relics of Saint Paul the Hermit to Hungary in 1381. Alsányi was named Cardinal of Saint Sabina in 1384.

We know that around 1389–1404 the Faculty of Canon and Civil Law was still functioning at the University of Pécs, because the pope granted the revenues of

the Collegiate Church of Saint John of Pécs and Saint
Peter of Pozsega in Croatia to the doctors of Canon and
Civil Law teaching in Pécs at the time[61].

A Collection of University Sermons Given at Pécs

An interesting literary document that sheds light on the
activities of the University of Pécs is a collection of
199 sermons compiled at the University (*Sermones
complilate in studio generali Quinqueecclesiensi in Regno
Ungarie*). It is not the original version but a fifteenth-
century copy executed in a German-speaking environment,
with German explanatory glosses and words inscribed
in the margins.

In my opinion, the sermons were originally pronounced
at the University of Pécs as part of the regular university
program, which demanded attendance at university
sermons. At such university sermons, the entire student
body and the Faculty had to be present, regardless
whether or not the University possessed a Faculty of
Theology. The word *compilatio* in our Collection indicates
that it was worked out as a scholastic exercise. In university teaching the *lectio* (lecture) was considered the
foundation of a building, the *disputatio* (dispute) the walls,
and the *predicatio* (sermons) the roof protecting the
faithful from the heat of summer and the hurricane of
vices[62].

The author must have been a Dominican: because he
emphasized the importance of Dominican Saints with

31

eight sermons on the founder of the Order. His Hungarian origin is above dispute for he recalled the memory of Saint Stephen[63] with nostalgia[64] (Plate no. 5). Another evidence of his Hungarian origin is that the memory and merits of Saint Adalbert were gratefully recalled as of the first missionary in converting Hungarians to Christianity[65]. Hungarian authorship is confirmed by his quoting the hymn *Laetare Pannonia* ("Rejoice Pannonia") from the Hungarian breviary and frequently referring to Hungary as "our kingdom"[66].

It is possible that the original collection of the Pécs sermons was carried in the bag of a student or master to Germany. Let us not forget that one of the subjects of the University of Pécs was a German scholar from Nürnberg, Hermannus Lurcz.

Once out of Hungary, the manuscript was copied and provided with explanatory marginal notes in German. The date of composition must fall in the first half of the fifteenth century.

One of the last sermons in the Collection, the one hundred ninety-eight, fittingly summarized the duties of university subjects, namely readers (teachers), students, and preachers[67]. The wealth of science was given by God to readers (teachers), students, and preachers[67]. From the teachers God expects profit from their frequent diligent and useful lectures (*lucrum lectionis*); from students He expects the gaining of enlightenment of the heart (*lucrum illuminationis cordis*) and assiduity in retaining in their memory what has been taught them; finally, from preachers God expects the emolument of the conversion of souls (*lucrum conversionis animarum*) if they preached

32

sincerely in the explanation of the Scriptures and in the commendation of virtues and condemnation of vices.

* * *

We do not know how long the University of Pécs existed. It must have been extinct by 1465, for the king of Hungary, Matthias Corvinus, on May 19 of that year informed Pope Paul II that there was no university in operation in the country[68] (Plate no. 6).

Proof of the survival of the University of Pécs in the fifteenth century, according to Petrovich, is that in 1431 and 1432 a student and *declinista* in the *schola Quinqueecclesiensis*—school of Pécs—, Ipolitus de Weresmarth, copied several theological treatises[69]. The copyst calls himself student and *declinista*[70]. This, in my opinion, does not mean that he was a Master teaching in a school because the word "student" is very explicit and *declinista*[71] means someone engaged in grammatical studies.

Petrovich did not know that six years later, in 1438, Ipolitus de Weresmarth matriculated at the University of Vienna, in the Hungarian Nation under Johannes Polczmacher, Doctor in Canon Law[72]. Until we have further proof that Ipolitus de Weresmarth meant the *University* when he spoke about studying in the *schola*, we cannot make definite statement about him being a subject at the University of Pécs functioning as such at that time.

We are inclined to accept the opinion of such historians as Ábel that the University of Pécs was not in full existence in the fifteenth century[73].

Fabian Igali, the former guardian at the Franciscan convent of Pécs, upon being elected Provincial, proposed in 1454 that four large monasteries of his Order have schools for the instruction of the young Franciscans and that the best of them be sent abroad because of the lack of universities in the country[74]. This confirms Matthias Corvinus's statement in a letter dated 1465 addressed to the Pope, that there was no university in the country: *non viget aliquod studium generale*[75].

We have evidence that on the 2nd of March 1494 the king of Hungary made a small grant to students in the *schola maior Quinqueecclesiensis*[76]. The question arises again: does *schola maior* refer to a university or to major cathedral school?

Several sixteenth-century chroniclers make definite mention of students in the school of Pécs without stating that they were students of a university. In the beginning of the sixteenth century, Paul Gregóriancz said that there were so many students in Pécs that one could have formed an army with them[77].

Nicholas Oláh, who later became Archbishop of Esztergom, early in his life spent six years in Pécs, from 1516 to 1522, as secretary of Bishop Szathmáry. In his description of this city, unfortunately he made no mention of the existence and functioning of a university[78].

The only important information about student life in Pécs in the sixteenth century is given by Nicholas [Miklós] Istvánffy, who was born in Pécs in 1538. He wrote about 2,000 students studying at the *gymnasium* of Pécs before 1532[79]. The puzzling question always remains: do *schola maior* or *gymnasium* necessarily mean a university, not just the cathedral or some other school? Basing our assumption upon the scanty information given by Istvánffy, we may conclude that the University survived until 1543.

The student of Pécs must have had splendid quarters, if we can believe a Turkish traveller, Evlia Cselebi. In 1664 in his description of Pécs, he spoke of the existence of a school, with 70 rooms, in the vicinity of the cathedral, in the castle in his time occupied by the Turkish army[80], information which may suggest that the University somehow survived till the middle of the sixteenth century in the modest form of a *hochschule*.

* * *

UNIVERSITAS ISTROPOLITANA,
THE UNIVERSITY OF POZSONY

A University of Short Duration:
Óbuda (Veterisbuda)

It is most unlikely that the University of Pécs was very active or even in existence by 1395, when Sigismund, king of Hungary (1382–1437), requested a papal charter for preparing the founding of the University of Óbuda. This "Sigismundean University" was not long-lived for it was extinct by 1403, probably uprooted by the revolt against Sigismund fomented by a former Paris master, Benedictus of Makra[81].

Sometime in 1409/10 Sigismund again petitioned Pope John XXIII (1410–1417) for the erection of a university in Hungary. The pope, in a letter to his papal legate, Branda of Piacenza, authorized him to look for a suitable location for the new university requested by Sigismund[82].

The bull of foundation for the new university, issued August 1, 1410, allowed the establishment of the Faculties of Theology, Civil and Canon Law, and Arts (*qualibet licita Facultate in oppido suo Veterisbude*), hoping that the university would propagate the faith, instruct the simple, serve equity, and increase good judgment[83]. He extended the same privileges to the subjects as those enjoyed by the Universities of Paris,

Bologna, Oxford, and Cologne. The provost of Buda was appointed chancellor.

A sizable delegation represented the University of Óbuda at the Council of Constance (1414), led by Lambert, chancellor of the University, provost of Óbuda, a canonist (Plate no. 7). Among the Hungarian members of the delegation was Tadeus de Vicomercato from Milan, a professor at the University of Padua[84]. The Hungarians were on a par with the illustrious emissaries of the Universities of Paris, Cologne, Vienna, Heidelberg, Prague, Orleans, London, Erfurt, Holdenburg [?], Avignon, Bologna, Cracow, and Oxford. The passage from Richental's *Chronicle* referring to the Sundens is the last information we have on the University of Óbuda. It is doubtful that it survived the death of its founder, Sigismund (1382–1437).

Petition of Matthias Corvinus to Pope Paul II

The light of learning in Hungary was rekindled by a great friend of letters and patron of humanism, Matthias Corvinus, King of Hungary (1458–1490), and his two high-ranking prelates: Johannes Vitéz, archbishop of Esztergom (appointed in 1465), and Janus Pannonius, the poet bishop of Pécs, who took possession of his see in 1459.

Corvinus's petition for the erection of a university was presented to Pope Paul II (1464–1471) in 1465 by Janus Pannonius, head of a Hungarian embassy to Rome, asking for the Pontiff's help against the menacing Turkish invasion into Hungary, rampart of western Christianity.

The presentation of the petition was recorded in the papal records on May 19, 1465 (Plate no. 6). Matthias Corvinus informed the pope that Hungary, though great and rich, had no university[85]. Students desirous to learn were forced to go abroad, exposed to long and perilous journeys and faced with the difficulty of learning new languages. Corvinus asked the pope for permission to establish a university of the Bologna type (*ad instar studii Bononiensis*), considerable advance over the organization of the Universities of Pécs and Óbuda[86].

Pope Paul authorized the establishment of the University on the same day, May 19, 1465, in a bull addressed not to the king but to the archbishop of Esztergom, Johannes Vitéz, and the bishop of Pécs, Janus Pannonius. The pope ordered Johannes Vitéz to draw up statutes for the planned university on the model of those of Bologna and left their validity to a further confirmation by the Holy See. Vitéz was vested with the same rights and privileges as those enjoyed by the chancellor of the University of Bologna. The pope did not specify the location of the University but left it up to the discretion of the king[87].

The New University Established in Pozsony

The choice fell on Pozsony (Pressburg in German; today Bratislava), on the banks of the Danube (Plate no. 8), 25 miles east of Vienna, a city second in importance to Buda at the time. The building which was to house the new University was donated by the king, a house that had belonged to Stephanus Gmaintl, a well-to-do burgher of Pozsony who died without heirs. The building was a combination of college (i.e., home for students) and university, with living quarters for students in one wing and classrooms in the other. A large and beautiful garden surrounded the building[88].

Chancellor Vitéz and the Organization of the University

The recruiting of professors was done by Johannes Vitéz, archbishop of Esztergom, himself. He informed the city of Pozsony of the coming of several professors, whom he had selected, to staff the new university: Johannes, a canonist and Master of Theology, Martinus, Master of Arts, and Petrus, Doctor in Medicine[89]. He also invited others from Italy and France.

Vitéz took upon himself the office of the chancellor. We may say that from this moment the university was almost identified with his personal prestige, success, and good fortune. He did not follow the text of the papal bull. The statutes of the university were not modeled after those of Bologna—where the rector, representative of the students, had the upper hand—but Vitéz rather followed the example of Vienna and Paris, for he believed that the strong hand of a chancellor was needed to run the university.

Advice from Vienna

Among the important scholars who complimented Vitéz on his wise decision to select Pozsony for the seat of the new university was the Austrian Dominican

Leonhard Huntpichler, of the University of Vienna and several times dean of the Faculty of Theology there. He begged the archbishop to follow the instructions of the Council of Basel (1431–1443) in the organization of the university, particularly in the matter of the conferring of benefices. The decree of the Council of Basel on the giving of benefices was not especially welcomed by universities because the Council put it in the hands of the bishops, who frequently disregarded the recommendation of the universities. The latter preferred the old system, whereby the *rotulus*—where the names of candidates were inscribed—was composed by the university and sent to the pope for the bestowing of the benefices.

The Austrian theologian also recommended *Nove alme universitatis hystropolensis supremo cancellario*, the teaching of both ways (*ambae viae*), the *via antiqua* and the *via moderna*, nominalist and realist philosophical system, a concept adopted at the time by the University of Heidelberg[90].

On April 26, 1469, Vitéz granted extensive jurisdiction to the provost of the Collegiate Chapter of Pozsony, Georgius Schönberg (died 1486), whom he named vice Chancellor. Vitéz did this in the interest of the subjects of the university, so that in certain juridical cases they would not be interrupted and abandon study and to recur to the authority of the archbishop in Esztergom[91]. The magnificent tombstone of Georgius Schönberg stands in the Gothic Church of Saint Martin in Pozsony, in all probability executed by Nicholas Gerhaert von Leyden, who made the sarcophagus of Frederick III in *Stefanskirche* in Vienna.

The most famous and celebrated scholar attracted to the *Universitas Istropolitana* of Pozsony was Johannes Müller, born in 1436 in Königsberg (Franconia); hence the latinized version of his name, *Regiomontanus*. At the age of twelve, he matriculated at the University of Leipzig, in 1447[92], and developed an early interest in astronomy. Lured by the reputation of Georgius Peuerbach, a famous scientist and a friend of Vitéz (died 1461), he went to the University of Vienna in 1450, where he became, in 1452, Bachelor of Arts and in 1457 Master of Arts[93]. His master quickly recognized the extraordinary talent of his pupil, and they became co-workers.

Cardinal Bessarion (1385–1472), envoy of Sixtus IV to Vienna, principal advocate of action against the Turks, convinced Regiomontanus in 1460 at Vienna to study Greek. In collaboration with his former master, Georgius Peuerbach, he translated Ptolemy's *Almagaste* into Latin. During his extended trip to Italy, he befriended the Polish astronomer Martinus Ilkusch. Both of them were invited to Hungary by Vitéz, who excelled in the art of convincing people, with his sweet voice that sounded like an organ[94].

Regiomontanus arrived at Esztergom, seat of the archbishop of Hungary, in 1467. In collaboration with Martinus Ilkusch, he drew up the horoscope of the new University of Buda in June 1467[95] (Plate no. 9).

The inauguration of the *Universitas Istropolitana* took place very soon afterwards. Regiomontanus taught the *quadrivium*, commuting frequently between the University of Pozsony and Esztergom for four years (1467–1471). During his stay in Hungary, he composed his *Tabulae directionum profectionumque nobilis*, which he dedicated to the benefactor of the university, his patron, Johannes Vitéz[96] (Plate no. 10). Sixty years before Copernicus, he taught that the earth moves around its axis.

In 1471 Vitéz and his nephew, Janus Pannonius, were involved in a plot against Matthias Corvinus (Plates nos. 11; 12; 13; 14). Disapproving of the foreign policy of the king and his imposition of heavy taxes, and resenting the increasing role of foreign clergy, both wanted to assure the passing on of the throne to a "legitimate" successor, Prince Casimir of Poland. When Matthias learned of the plot, he had Vitéz and his nephew arrested. Vitéz died shortly afterwards, in 1471, and his nephew fled to Croatia and died in the castle of the bishop of Zagreb in 1472.

When his protector was exiled, Regiomontanus left Hungary. He was called to Rome by Pope Sixtus IV in 1475 in the reform of the calendar. He died there, fairly young, forty years old, and is buried in the Pantheon.

Martinus Ilkusch, *Royal Astrologer*, *Plebanus of Buda*

Martinus Ilkusch, through the connections of his Cracow master, Martinus Król of Zurawica, belonged to the scientific circle of Peuerbach's student, Regiomontanus. Master of Arts in 1459, from Cracow Ilkusch went to Padua, Italy, in 1463, where he met Regiomontanus. After a short interval of teaching in Bologna, we find him in Rome, where he was awarded the office of court astrologer by the newly elected Pope Paul II. In Rome he met the Hungarian humanist bishop, Janus Pannonius, who was conducting negotiations for the foundation of a university in Hungary.

He went to Esztergom in the company of Regiomontanus, collaborating with the latter in the composition of the above-mentioned *Tabulae*, written in the castle of Esztergom[97].

Martinus Ilkusch arrived at Pozsony on July 20, 1467, where he was received with a superb banquet offered by the city fathers for the *Toktores*—delicious chicken, fish, meat, hot cakes, and wine—to open the university: *um di Hochschule anzuheben*[98].

Matthias Corvinus used Ilkusch's services frequently, and sent for him even during his campaigns, as on July 28, 1468, when he requested Ilkusch's presence at Hradistye in Bohemia which the king was besieging.

When, on September 22, 1468, a comet appeared over the city of Pozsony, he set forth to compose a treatise on the phenomenon, which he dedicated to the king on October 6, predicting all kinds of ills for Frederick II, Louis XI of France, and Casimir of Poland. He signed it as *archidiaconus Zagrabiensis ecclesie*, which signature shows that the had been generously provided with benefices by the king[99].

In 1471, after the death of the chancellor, Johannes Vitéz, he followed Regiomontanus's example, and left Pozsony for Buda. On January 11, 1472, on the occasion of the appearance of a comet over Buda, he composed another astrological treatise on this phenomenon and ascribed it to King Matthias Corvinus, signing himself *plebanus Budensis*. During his stay at Buda, he remained a faithful companion to the king. When Matthias Corvinus besieged Vienna in 1485 and received the homage of the university, the official register of the Faculty of Arts reports that Martinus Ilkusch interceded for the university's obtaining the good graces of the king[100].

Martinus Ilkusch remained in Hungary even after the death of Matthias (1490). Faithful alumnus of his old University of Cracow, he sent his books and astronomical instruments—a celestial globe, a *torquetus*, and two astrolabes—to Cracow before his death, around 1493 to 1494.

Theologians, Canonists, and Philosophers Teaching at Pozsony

Among the professors mentioned in the letter of Johannes Vitéz to the City of Pozsony was a certain *Johannes*, Doctor in Canon Law and Master in Theology, who can most probably be identified with the Dominican Johannes Gattus, known for his defeat by Matthias during a disputation. Once, dining with the king and influenced by good Hungarian wine, the Italian theologian boasted that there was not a question that he could not answer. The king challenged him, asking: If God was such a just Being as theologians teach, how could it be that John the Evangelist, without any sin, was not chosen to head Christ's Church but that the sinner, Peter, was preferred? All that the Dominican could answer was that the reasoning of God is inscrutable. Hereupon Matthias asked for the text of Saint Jerome against Jovinian and proved from it that Saint Peter was elevated to the primacy in order to show God's intention, that the sinful mankind can be lifted from its corruption[101].

Another professor teaching at Pozsony was Laurentius Koch de Krompach (Krumpach), former procurator of the Hungarian Nation at the University of Vienna and a Theologian. He read the *Sencences* of Peter Lombard[102]. On October 20, 1469, Johannes Vitéz asked the Faculty of Theology in Vienna for a dispensation in favor or Laurentius Koch de Krompach, allowing him to satisfy the requirements for his degree by lecturing on the *Sentences* at the University of Pozsony[103]. When Vitéz fell in disgrace with the king, Laurentius returned to Vienna.

Another distinguished scholar who taught in Pozsony was Nicholaus Schrickher de Hittendorf, from the diocese of Passau, who was dean of the Faculty of Arts of the University of Vienna in 1456 and 1460. He was in Pozsony in 1470. Stephanus Murer de Brunn, the very same year, asked the Faculty of Arts to send a certain book, to be used as exemplar, to Nicholas de Hittendorf lecturing at the University of Pozsony[104].

Around 1470 Paul, archdeacon of Mosony, Johannes de Cracovia, dean of the Faculty of Arts, and Johannes Kuppferberth, Master of Arts, were at the University of Pozsony[105].

Students

A student–bursa or hostel was also functioning at the University of Pozsony, where around 1479 we find such Hungarian names as Benedictus Polýan, Ludovicus de Pákos, Johannes de Szentmihály, Johannes de Szentgyörgy (Plate no. 15). Archive material reveals that Johannes Lökös spent some time at the university accompanied by his tutor[106].

With the departure of such important professors as Regiomontanus and Ilkusch, several bachelors of the University of Pozsony transferred to the University of Vienna. On October 13, 1471, Petrus Forhinger de Kirchdorff, *baccalarius Posoniensis*, and on April 14, 1473, Martinus de Weytra, *baccalarius Histropolensis*, were received into the Austrian Nation, and Johannes Flechtner de Hirsberg, *baccalarius Histropolensis*, also on April 14, 1473, into the Hungarian Nation of the University of Vienna[107].

Decline

After 1471 the number of native students from Pozsony registered at the University of Vienna increased. This is another sign of the decline of the activities of the University of *Istropolitana*. On October 13, 1470, Ludovicus Anwein, on April 14, 1471, Martinus Tuerk, Bernardinus Roemer, Wolfgangus Tinctoris, and Johannes Snellhart all from Pozsony (*de Posonio*), were in Vienna. On April 14, 1472, Christoforus Arcuficis and Johannes Holtzapfl; on April 14, 1473, Wenzeslaus Anwein; on April 14, 1473, Johannes Thebin, Thomas Weyss, and Laurencius Fabri, all from Pozsony (*de Posonio*)[108], were admitted into the *Studium* of Vienna.

All the important professors seem to have left by the time of the death of Vitéz on August 10, 1492, but the University of Pozsony continued to function. A scant sign that life was still there is the fact that the Italian

47

humanist, Thaddeus Ugoletti, bought some books for Pozsony[109].

After the death of King Matthias Corvinus, the university became a dying institution. In 1492 part of the university building was given away by King Wladislas II to Blasius Pósa, who married the great-granddaughter of the original owner, Gmaintl. The other part was transformed into an armory, and displaced stones were used in rebuilding the neighboring city tower *Schusterthurm*[110].

Tradition and Present Reality

Pozsony did not disappear from the scene of Hungarian higher education (Plate no. 16). On May 12, 1635, Cardinal Pázmány, archbishop of Esztergom with 60,000 florins in his possession, signed the foundation charter of the University of Nagyszombat (*Tyrnaviensis*), a step taken for the revival of the cultural assets of his country, devastated by the Turks (*patriae charissimae sublevanda*).

The name of Pozsony was again in the limelight because the Cardinal of the Counter Reform hesitated for a while between Pozsony and Nagyszombat. In the deed of foundation, he stipulated that after the liberation of the country from Turkish occupation, the university could be transferred to another city of the kingdom. Therefore, a new university was founded by Cardinal Pázmány, archbishop of Esztergom, a successor of Johannes Vitéz.

The university was given new splendor by Maria Theresia in 1769 when she took the university under her royal patronage. In the year of the publication of the

Ratio educationis, on August 22, 1777, the university was transferred to Budapest. It was opened on November 3, 1777, with *Veni, sancte spiritus*, in the Church of Our Lady, near the old University of Buda (Plate no. 17). The solemn opening was to take place on the birthday of Maria Theresia, May 13, 1778, but it actually occurred on June 25. The names of Pozsony and Cardinal Pázmány were connected intimately with the foundation of the University of Budapest and the two names always remained inseparable[111].

In 1626 Pázmány built a palace for the Jesuits in Pozsony, which later became the Academy of Law. In the same palace, in 1914, a new university, named after the wife of Franz Joseph, Queen Elizabeth, was founded. After the peace treaty of Trianon in 1921, the Queen Elizabeth University was transferred to Pécs. Through the irony or fancy of history, a chain of events seems hidden in the blood circulation of present-day Hungarian universities. The new universities willingly and knowingly followed the path of historical tradition. The University of Pécs of 1967 came from Pozsony, a favorite place of Vitéz, archbishop of Esztergom, The existence of the University of Buda was due to a generous gesture of another archbishop of Esztergom, Cardinal Pázmány.

The souvenir of the old University of Pozsony is embodied in the foundation charter of the University of Budapest. Its founder, Cardinal Pázmány (died 1637) lies buried in the Church of Saint Martin of Pozsony where Regiomontanus, Martinus Ilkusch, and Johannes Vitéz listened to the opening sermon of the *Universitas Istropolitana* half a millenium ago.

For the past, present, and future students of my old Alma Mater, Cardinal Pázmány Péter University of Budapest, I have a message which I read on the plane coming to deliver this lecture[112]: *La mémoire est une maison vide dans laquelle chacun pénètre un jour ou l'autre avec sa charge de souvenirs*—Memory is an empty house which everyone enters sooner or later with the heavy burden of his souvenirs*.

Astrik L. Gabriel
The Mediaeval Institute
The University of Notre Dame
Notre Dame, Indiana

* Lecture given in honor of The 600th Anniversary of Hungarian University Education on December 16, 1967, at The Carnegie Endowment for International Peace, New York, N. Y., sponsored by The New York American Hungarian Federation.

NOTES

[1] D. Dercsényi, F. Pogány, Z. Szentkirályi, *Pécs* [The City of Pécs] (Városképek-Műemlékek, Pécs), Budapest, 1956.

[2] S. Borovszky, ed., Pozsony vármegye (Magyarország vármegyéi és városai) [Comitat of Pozsony]: Bratislava, Budapest, s. d., P. von Ballus, *Presburg und seine Umgebung*, Presburg, 1823.

[3] D. Dercsényi, *Nagy Lajos kora* [The Century of Louis the Great, King of Hungary], Budapest, s. d.

[4] A. L. Gabriel, *Les rapports dynastiques franco-hongrois au moyen-âge*, Budapest, 1944, 35–51.

[5] German translation: M. Kálti, *Die Ungarische Bilderchronik*, *Chronica de Gestis Hungarorum*, Berlin, Rütten and Loening, 1961;—Latin text in E. Szentpétery, ed., *Scriptores rerum hungaricarum*, Budapest, I–II, 1937–38, pp. 215–505.

[6] D. G. Kosáry, *A History of Hungary*, Cleveland, 1941, p. 46.

[7] *Ibid.*, p. 55.

[8] H. Grundmann, "Sacerdotium, Regnum, Studium", *Archiv für Kulturgeschichte*, 34 (1951) 5–21.

[9] G. de Lagarde, *La naissance de l'esprit laïque au déclin du Moyen âge, II, Marsile de Padoue ou le premier théoricien de l'état laïque*, Paris, 1948, pp. 264–270; A. Gewirth, *Marsilius of Padua, The Defender of Peace*, New York, 1951, 1956, 2 vols.

[10] "Tota communitas cleri cujusvis conditionis et status regni predicti careat et caruerit ab antiquo honore magistrali theologice facultatis": H. Denifle–Ae. Chatelain, ed., *Chartularium Universitatis Parisiensis*, I–IV, Paris, 1889–1897, II, p. 570, no. 1114.

[11] *Chart. Univ. Paris.*, III, p. 20, no. 1216.

[12] *Ibid.*, III, p. 20, no. 1216, note.

[13] R. W. Seton-Watson, *Prague Essays Presented by a Group of British Historians to the Caroline University of Prague on the Occasion of Its Six-Hundredth Anniversary*, Oxford, 1949, p. 53.

[14] F. Gall, *Alma Mater Rudolphina 1365–1965, Die Wiener Universität und Ihre Studenten*, Wien, 1965.

[15] "Quae in Studiis generalibus, videlicet Bononiensi et Paduano tenentur et observantur": *Codex Diplomaticus Universitatis Studii Generalis Cracoviensis, Pars Prima =* 1365–1440 = Cracow, 1870, I. p. 1, no. I.

[16] *Ibid.*, p. 6, no. III.

[17] F. Gall, "Gründung und Anfänge der Wiener Universität", *Les universités européennes du XIVe au XVIIIe siècle. Aspects et Problèmes* (Institut d'Histoire de la Faculté des Lettres de l'Université de Genève no. 4), Genève, 1967, pp. 48–55.

[18] E. Kovács, "Die Gründung der Universität Pécs und Ihre Bedeutung für die Ungarische Kultur", *Les universités européennes du XIVe au XVIIIe siècle*, Genève, 1967, p. 39, note 10.

[19] "Ut ibidem fides ipsa dilatetur, erudiantur simplices, equitas servetur, iudicii crescat ratio et intellectus huiusmodi augeatur": R. Békefi, *A Pécsi Egyetem*, Budapest, 1909, p. 15, col. 2.

[20] A. Vetulani, "A pécsi egyetem, valamint a krakkói és bécsi testvéregyetemek alapításának körülményei" [Les circonstances accompagnant la fondation de l'Université de Pécs et ses universités-soeurs de Cracovie et de Vienne], Csizmadia, A., ed., *A Pécsi Egyetem Történetéből* [From the History of the University of Pécs], Pécs, 1967, pp. 24–25.

His reference to Colle, *Storia Scientifico-letteraria dello Studio di Padova*, 4 vols., Padova, 1824–25, Vol. II, on page 25, note 8, should be corrected to Vol. II. 146.

[21] A. Csizmadia, "Galvano di Bologna pécsi müködése és a középkori magyar jogi oktatás egyes kérdései" [The Activities of Galvanus of Bologna at Pécs and Some Problems in the Teaching of Law in Medieval Hungary], Csizmadia, A., ed., *A pécsi Egyetem történetéből* [From the History of the University of Pécs] (Jubileumi Tanulmányok), Pécs, 1967, 111–128.

[22] *PL.* 141, col. 189, no. I.

[23] D. Simonyi, "Pécs 'Quinque Ecclesiae' nevének eredetéről" [The Origin of the Name of Pécs 'Quinque Ecclesiae'], *Antik Tanulmányok. Studia Antiqua*, 6 (1959) 87–103.

[24] "Tamquam insigniori et magis ad hoc accomada et idonea": Békefi, *A Pécsi Egyetem* [University of Pécs], p. 15, 22.

[25] "Ad multiplicanda doctrine semina et germina salutaria producenda": *ibid.*, p. 17.

[26] A. Veress, *Matricula et Acta Hungarorum in Universitatibus Italiae studentium 1221–1864* (Monumenta Hungariae Italica no. 3), Budapestini, 1941, p. 148.

[27] Died as archbishop of Kalocsa. *Ibid.*, pp. 2–3.

[28] *Ibid.*, p. 10.

[29] *Ibid.*, p. 395.

[30] "Charissimo in Christo filio Ludovico regi Ungarie illustri": Békefi, *A Pécsi Egyetem* [University of Pécs], p. 22, col. 2.

[31] "Alioquin prefate nostre littere nullius essent roboris vel momenti": *Vativan Archives*, Reg. Vat. vol. 256, fol. 681 verso.

[32] "Pro communi servicio Domini nostri Summi Pontificis et Sacri Collegii Dominorum Cardinalium": J. Koller, *Historia episcopatus Quinqueecclesiarum*, Posonii, 1784, Tomus III, pp. 86–89.

[33] *Ibid.*, p. 89.

[34] S. Kozlowska-Budkowa – F. Kavka – E. Kovács – F. Gall – S. Stelling-Michaud – E. Garin – J. Le Goff – W. A. Pantin – M. Steinmetz – B. Lesnodorski – G. A. Novicky, *Les universités européennes du XIVe au XVIIIe siècle. Aspects et Problèmes* (Institut d'Histoire de la Faculté des Lettres de Genève no. 4), Genève, 1967, p. 58.

[35] R. Békefi, *A Pécsi Egyetem* [University of Pécs], pp. 124 to 125.

[36] "Universis Doctoribus Magistris et scolaribus studii Quinqueecclesiensis": Koller, *Historia episcopatus Quinqueecclesiarum*, III, pp. 178–180; Békefi, *A Pécsi Egyetem* [University of Pécs], p. 129.

[37] "Ad residendum interim in Ecclesiis ipsis minime teneamini": Koller, *ibid.*, III, p. 179.

[38] *Ibid.*, III, p. 181.

[39] Dercsényi-Pogány-Szentkirályi, *Pécs*, p. 59.

[40] Alain, *Propos, sur le bonheur*, Paris Gallimard, 1928, pp. 180–181.

[41] "Qui in studio Quinqueeclesien. jura Canonica tunc actu legebas, sibi & sue Quinqueecclesien. Ecclesie multa grata servitia impenderas ... tibi provisionem annuam trecentarum marcharum argenti, seu sexcentorum flor. auri percipiendam & habendam ... et ... villam de Yruch ... & domum quam in Civitate Quinqueeclesien. inhabitas ...": Koller, *Historia episcopatus Quinqueeclesiarum*, Posonii, 1784, III, pp. 129–131.

[42] "Item ex nunc salariamus sedes infrascriptas, videlicet sedem Decretorum de quadraginta marcis argenti annuatim, sedem Decretalium de totidem": *Codex Dipl. Univ. Cracov.*, I, p. 3, no. 1.

[43] Csizmadia, "Galvano di Bologna", *A Pécsi Egyetem Történetéből* [From the History of the University of Pécs], p. 111.

[44] "Dilectus filius Galvanus de Bononia decretorum doctor adeo hactenus iuris canonici studiis laudabiliter insudavit ... et deinde in ipso Paduano et Quinqueecclesiensi studiis legit laudabiliter et ordinarie decretales": Reg. Vat. 285, fol. 115 recto. Edited by Békefi, *A Pécsi Egyetem* [University of Pécs], p. 128, no. IX [Plate no 3].

[45] L. Hain, *Repertorium Bibliographicum*, Berlin, 1925, no. 15601; 7452.

[46] Vat. Lat. 2683, ff. 225 r–227 r; F. M. Colle *Storia Scientifico-letteraria dello Studio di Padova*, Padova, Vol. III, p. 51; J. F. von Schulte, *Die Geschichte der Quellen und Literatur des Canonischen Rechts von der Mitte des 16. Jahrhunderts bis zur Gegenwart* (Die Geschichte der Quellen und Literatur des Canonischen Rechts von Gratian bis auf die Gegenwart, III), Stuttgart, 1880, II, p. 288; another work, *Casus, qui Judicis arbitrio reliquuntur*, is also in the Vatican Library, Vat. Lat. 2660, fol. 100 verso bis 106 verso; Csizmadia, *A pécsi Egyetem történetéből* [From the History of the University of Pécs], pp. 116–117.

[47] "Item in vigilia Trinitatis receptus fuit mag. Hermannus Lurcz de studio Quinclesiensi. d." [1379]: *Liber decanorum Facultatis Philosophicae Universitatis Pragensis, ab anno Christi 1397 usque ad annum 1585*, Pars I (Monumenta historica Universitatis Carolo-Ferdinandeae Pragensis, Tome I),

Prague, 1830 [Abbreviated *Mon. Univ. Prag.*] I, p. 186; cf. F. Kavka, "A prágai Károly egyetem, a pécsi egyetem és Dél-Magyarország a XIV. században és a XV század elején" [The University of Charles of Prague, the University of Pécs, and Southern Hungary in the XIVth and the Beginning of the XVth Centuries], Csizmadia, A., ed., *A pécsi Egyetem történetéből* [From the History of the University of Pécs] (Jubileumi Tanulmánok, Pécs, 1967, p. 88.

[48] "Item N. Heylprunna et Jo. de Crustantia facti sunt Baccalarii sub. mag. Hermanno Lurcze, dd." "Item 3. feria post Laetare det. Frider. Rabenolt sub mag. Lurcz.": *Mon. Univ. Prag.* I, p. 193.

[49] "Item eodem die det. Jo. Zaran de Wratislauia sub. mag. Hermannus Lurcz": *ibid.*, I, p. 206.

[50] "Hermannus Luercz de Nuernberga, magister in artibus, doctor in medicina et baccalarius in theologia, rector parrochialis ecclesie Holfeld Bambergensis diocesis, fuit electus in rectorem universitatis Wiennensis": [F. Gall], *Die Matrikel der Universität Wien, 1377–1450* (Publikationen des Instituts für Österreichische Geschichtsforschung), Graz-Köln, 1956, I. Band, p. 22.

[51] J. Lang, *Die Christologie bei Heinrich von Langenstein* (Freiburger Theologische Studien 85), Freiburg-Basel-Wien, 1966, p. 19–30; J. Aschbach, *Geschichte der Wiener Universität im ersten Jahrhunderte ihres Bestehens. Festschrift zu ihrer fünfhundertjährigen Gründungsfeier*, Wien, 1865, pp. 366 bis 402.

From Vienna he went to the University of Erfurt, 1396 rector, died there probably in 1399: E. Kleineidam, *Universitas Studii Erffordensis*. Teil I: 1392–1460, Leipzig, 1964, p. 27; 265–266.

[52] M. Denis, *Codices Manuscripti Theologici Bibliothecae Palatinae Vindobonensis Latini*, Vindobonae, 1795, Vol. I Pars III, p. 2565; Aschbach, *Geschichte der Wiener Universität*, p. 410, cf. 31; 53; 120; 133.

[53] "Non obstantibus quibuscumque privilegiis ac statutis et consvetudinibus studii Quinqueecclesiensis": Békefi, *A Pécsi Egyetem* [University of Pécs], p. 127, Reg. Aven. 170, fol. 541 recto.

[54] Petrus de Wydera (de Quinque-ecclesiis):

1384, July 3: received into the Faculty of Arts, "Item Petrus de Wydera baccalarius Quinque-ecclesiarum 3. die Julii est assumtus ad facultatem, d," *Mon. Univ. Prag.* I, p. 243.

1396: admitted to the baccalaureate, "Item in quadragesima in quatuor temporibus electi fuerunt examinatores baccalariandorum mag. Andreas de Zelenecz, Joannes Hildissen, Henricus Berlin, Paulus Wladimiri et admiserunt illos secundum ordinem: ... Petrus de Quinque-ecclesiis. dd", *ibid.*, p. 310.

1396: determined under Joannes Artsen, "Item dominica Laetare Petrus de Quinque-ecclesiis det. sub mag. Joanne Artsen", *ibid.*, p. 311 Joannes Artsen [alias Joannes de Langevelt de natione Bavarorum] was Dean of the Faculty of Arts, April 19, 1392, *ibid.*, p. 276.

[55] Stephanus de Quinque-ecclesiis:

1375: "Dns. Joannes Comes de Hohenloch, canonicus Babenbergensis, rector universitatis juristarum Pragens. anno Domini 1375 intitulavit subsequentes: ... Item Stephanus, canonicus Pont. et Quinque-eccl." This information is contained in the records of the Bavarian Nation, *Mon. Univ. Prag.* II/1, pp. 61–62.

[56] Andreas de Quinque-ecclesiis was admitted to the baccalaureate in the beginning of Lent in 1385 under the following masters: Joan de Moravia, Heningus de Borgh, Frider. Veltprecher, et Henr. Storch. *Mon. Univ. Prag.* I/1, p. 228.

Stephanus de Seremia (sive de Syrimia) was admitted to the baccalaureate during the Ember days following Pentecost in 1385. On July 10 he performed his *determinacio* under Johannes de Buda. "Item 10. die Julii det. Steph. de Syrimia sub mag. Jo. de Buda": *ibid.*, I/1, pp. 231–232.

Johannes Zaran (Zaraw) de Wratislavia performed his *determinacio* under Hermannus Lurcz on March 18, 1382. *Ibid.*, I/1, p. 206.

[57] *Bullae Bonifacii IX. P. M. pars altera. 1396–1404.* (Monumenta Vaticana historiam Regni Hungariae illustrantia), Budapest, 1889. Series I. Tomus IV, p. 219, no. 272.

[58] "... ipse Lucas cum quodam cultello et dictus acolitus cum quodam flagello, quos in manibus habebant luderent, contigit, quod, dum sic fraternaliter et amicabiliter invicem

56

luderent, dictus Lucas eundem acolitum non ex proposito aut ex cogitata malitia aut invidia seu malo zelo, sed casualiter sic ludendo in brachio paululum sine tamen sanguinis effusione percussit ... idemque acolitus circa finem vite sue asseruit, se potius ex alia infirmitate mortis periculum incursurum, quam ex predicta ludi percussione", *ibid.*, IV, pp. 412–413, no. 471.

[59] "S'en retournaissent tout courtoisement et en paix ... Neantmoins ... plusieurs autres escoliers ... armez les aucuns de cotez de fer et d'espées, les autres de bastons de pierres, coeffetez e leurs testez et d'autres armeures": *Chart. Univ. Paris.* III, p. 136–37, no. 1311.

[60] "Ac ecclesiastice persone tam religiose quam seculares, nec non Duces, Marchiones, Comites, Barones, Milites, Nobiles et laici ... communia civitatum, Universitatum, Oppidorum Castrorum, Villarum": Koller, *Historia episcopatus Quinqueecclesiarum*, III, p. 182.

[61] "Pro singulis Doctoribus Juris Canonici vel Civilis Quinqueecclesien. legentibus": Koller, *Historia episcopatus Quinqueecclesiarum*, III, pp. 380–81.

[62] "Quasi tectum est tegens fideles ab aestu et a turbine vitiorum": M. Davy, *Les sermons universitaires Parisiens de 1250–1251. Contribution à l'histoire de la prédication médiévale* (Etudes de Philosophie Médiévale no. 15), Paris, 1931, p. 24.

[63] "Sanctum regem nostrum Stephanum": München CLM 22363, fol. 67 recto, col. 1. On the upper margin: "De sancto Rege, Stephano Hungarie Dalmacie ac Croacie etc. Sermo".

[64] "Qualis fuit apud nos rex noster sanctus Stephanus" [second sermon on Saint Stephen] CLM 22363, fol. 68 recto: col. 1.

[65] "Minesterio sancti Adalberti cui honor a nobis detur, quia fuit nostrae conversionis primus propugnator": CLM 22363, fol. 69 verso, col. 1.

[66] "Regnum nostrum": *ibid.*, fol. 69 verso, col. 1.

[67] "Pecuniam scientiae dedit Deus lectoribus, studentibus, praedicatoribus ...": CLM 22363, fol. 151 verso, col. 1; cf. also E. Petrovich, "A pécsi egyetemi beszédgyűjtemény" [A Collection of Sermons Given at the University of Pécs], Csizmadia, A., ed., *A pécsi Egyetem történetéből* [From the History of the University of Pécs] (Jubileumi Tanulmányok), Pécs, 1967, p. 214.

[68] "Non viget aliquod studium generale": Békefi, *A Pécsi Egyetem* [University of Pécs], p. 48; Vatican Archives, Reg. Suppl. 581, fol. 55 verso–56 recto (Plate no. 6).

[69] E. Petrovich, "A középkori pécsi egyetem megszűnése [Wie lange bestand die mittelalterliche Universität in Pécs?], *Janus Pannonius Múzeum*, 1966, pp. 153–170.

[70] "Expliciunt dicta sanctorum patrum de sollemnitatibus missarum per manus Ipoliti de Weresmarth studentis ac decliniste Quinqueecclesiensis, nati Ambrosi de Senthgwrgh. Et finali determinatione sunt determinata feria sexta ante dominicam sequentem post Octavam Pasche, videlicet Misericordia Domini, in scola predicte civitatis. De quorum dictorum utilitatibus actor fuit affectans incipiendo, sed magis est gaudens finiendo. Anno Domini MCCCCXXX primo." Wien, Cod. 3979 fol. 89 recto.

[71] "Explicit tabula preceptorum per divinam prudentiam in monte Synai Moysi traditorum omnibus fidelibus devote servare et venerare feria tertia post Epiphaniam immediate sequenti per manus Ipoliti de Weresmarth decliniste in scola Quinqueecclesiensi anno a Nativitate Domini Millesimo Quadringentesimo Tricesimo 2-o ante Vesperarum sollemnitatem hora quasi tertia a prima. Scriptor huius fuit valde delectabilis de presenti materia, quia utilis, auxilietur mihi virtus Spiritus Sancti. Amen." [I am giving an improved text of Petrovich's reading of the colophon. Several words were left out from the text as published by him.] Wien, Cod. 3979 fol. 113 verso.

[72] [F. Gall], *Die Matrikel der Universität Wien, 1377–1450* (Publikationen des Instituts für Österreichische Geschichtsforschung), Graz-Köln, 1956. I. Band, p. 205. Paid 4 gr.

[73] J. Ábel, *Egyetemeink a középkorban* [Hungarian Universities in the Middle Ages], Budapest, 1881, pp. 13–41.

[74] J. Karácsonyi, *Szt. Ferencz Rendjének története Magyarországon 1711-ig* [The History of the Franciscan Order in Hungary till 1711], Budapest, 1922, Vol. I, p. 64.

[75] See note 68, Békefi, *A Pécsi Egyetem* [University of Pécs], p. 48; Vatican Archives, Reg. Suppl. 581, fol. 55 verso to 56 recto (Plate no. 6).

[76] "Secundo die Marcii ad relacionem Bradach scolaribus schole majoris Quinqueecclesiensis dedi fl. III": J. Koller,

Historia episcopatus Quinqueecclesiarum, Posonii, 1796, To-mus IV, p. 483; R. Békefi, *A Pécsi Egyetem* [University of Pécs], p. 49.

[77] E. Petrovich, "A középkori Pécsi Egyetem megszünése" [Wie lange bestand die mittelalterliche Universität in Pécs?], p. 164, note 43.

[78] *Nicolai Olahi metropolitae Strigoniensis Hungaria et Atila sive de originibus gentis, regni Hungariae situ, habitu, opportu-nitatibus et rebus bello paceque ab Atila gestis libri duo*, Vindo-bonae, 1763, pp. 37–38.

[79] "Fuit etiam olim in ea gymnasium litterarum haud ince-lebre, tanto juvenum studiosorum concursu, ut paucis ante hoc bellum annis, duo milia eorum in ea numerata fuisse feran-tur": N. [M.] Istvánffy, *Regni Hungarici Historia per Nicolaum Isthuanffium Pannonium, ejusdem Regni Propalatinum libris XXXIV. exacte descripta*, Cologne, 1685, p. 170.

[80] E. Bako—M. J. Horváth, *Six Hundred Years of Hungarian University Education. Catalog*, College Park, Maryland, 1967, pp. 5–6; R. Békefi, *A Pécsi Egyetem* [University of Pécs] pp. 61–62; E. Petrovich, "A középkori Pécsi Egyetem megszü-nése" [Wie lange bestand die mittelalterliche Universität in Pécs?], p. 167, note 55.

[81] A. L. Gabriel, *Magyar diákok és tanárok a középkori Párizsban* [La vie à Paris des étudiants hongrois au moyen âge], Budapest, 1938, pp. 15–16; K. Heilig, "Zur Geschichte der ältesten ungarischen Universitäten und des Magisters Benedikt von Makra", *Jahrbuch des Wiener ungarischen Historischen Instituts* I (1431), 41–49).

[82] "Super dicte loci idoneitate et aliis circumstanciis invene-ris": A. Theiner, *Vetera Monumenta Historiae Hungariae Sacrae Illustrata*, Rome, 1860, II, p. 184; G. Bónis, "Einflüsse des römischen Rechts in Ungarn", *Ius Romanum Medii Aevi*, Pars V, 10, Milano, 1964, p. 44.

[83] L. S. Domonkos, *A History of Three Early Hungarian Universities: Óbuda, Pozsony, and Buda. Dissertation.* The Mediaeval Institute, Notre Dame, Indiana, 1966 (In typescript), pp. 10–28.

[84] [Ulrich von Richental], *Das Concilium So zu Constanz gehalten ist worden*, Heinrich Stainer, ed., (Augsburg, 1536). *Ulrich von Richental* "Chronik des Constanzer Concils 1414

bis 1418, Text der Aulendorfer Handschrift, Unveränderter Neudruck der von Richard Michael Buck besorgten Ausgabe, 1936 (F. W. Hendel Verlag zu Meersburg am Bodensee und Leipzig), fol. CXXII verso.

[85] "In regno Ungarie, licet amplo et fertili, non viget aliquod studium generale": Vatican Archives Reg. Suppl. 581, fol. 55 verso–56 recto (Plate no. 6).

[86] Vatican Archives, Reg. Suppl. 581, fol. 56; Békefi, *A Pécsi Egyetem* [University of Pécs], p. 131, no. 16: "Quibus dictum studium Bononiense et illius cancellarius, doctores et scolares ac promoti pro tempore gaudent et utuntur".

[87] "Quod ipse Rex ad id aptam seu aptum duxerit eligendam seu eligendum": Koller, *Historia episcopatus Quinqueecclesiarum*, Posonii, 1796, IV, pp. 146–148.

[88] J. Ábel, *Egyetemeink a középkorban* [Hungarian Universities in the Middle Ages], p. 29, notes 33–34.

[89] "Joannes miseracione divina Archi-Episcopus Strigoniensis, locique ejusdem Comes perpetuus, Primas hungarie et Apostolice sedis legatus natus, Prudentibus viris Magistro Civium, Judici ac Juratis Civibus Civitatis Posoniensis salutem, Credimus vos non ignorare, quod ex concessione Sedis Apostolice, et voluntate serenissimi domini nostri Regis institutum sit studium generale in illa Civitate, et ob eam causam de voluntate domini nostri Regis transmisimus hinc doctores ante omnia venerabilem fratrem JOHANNEM doctorem decretorum, et magistrum sacre Theologie, et item magistrum MARTINUM, doctorem Arcium, preterea magistrum PETRUM doctorem Arcium et medicine, ut iam Domino annuente, in illa universitate, id quod institutum est executioni demandetur, incipiantque lectiones. Brevi etiam temporis venturi sunt et alii doctores, pro quibus conducendis, partim ad Italiam, partim ad Franciam misimus ... ": this letter of Johannes Vitéz to the elders of Pozsony was edited first by Carolus Theoph. Windisch and published among others in G. A. Belnay, *Historia Literarum Bonarumque artium in Hungaria e probatissimis Scriptoribus synoptice deducta*, Viennae – Posonii – Cassoviae – Pestini, 1799, pp. 37–38.

[90] Vatican Library, Cod. Ottobon. Lat. no. 689, fol. 131 recto–142 recto; I. W. Frank. O. P., "Leonhard Huntpichler

O. P. († 1478) Theologieprofessor und Ordensreformer in Wien", *Archivum Fratrum Praedicatorum*, 36 (1966) pp. 338 bis 340; cf. G. Ritter, *Studien zur Spätscholastik* (Sitzungsberichte der Heidelberger Akademie der Wissenschaften, Philosophisch-historische Klasse, 1922, Abhandlung 7), II; *Via antiqua und via moderna auf den deutschen Universitäten des XV. Jahrhunderts*, Heidelberg, 1922.

[91] "Pro commodo et melio ac salubri statu Venerabilium doctorum nec non magistrorum et studentium in hac Universitate studii generalis Hystropolitani de novo instituti, pro tempore commorancium, ne iidem relictis studiis eorum in casibus vel causis emergentibus ad nos seu sedem nostram semper recurrere cogantur": Ábel, *Egyetemeink a középkorban* [Hungarian Universities in the Middle Ages], p. 76.

[92] G. Erler, *Die Matrikel der Universität Leipzig, Die Immatrikulationen von 1409–1559*, Leipzig, Giesecke and Devrient, 1895, I, p. 161, line 15: "Iohannes Molitoris, x gr.".

[93] Aschbach, *Geschichte der Wiener Universität*, p. 538.

[94] J. Horváth, *Az Irodalmi Műveltség Megoszlása* [History of Hungarian Literature in the Renaissance Period], Budapest, 1944, pp. 67–69–74.

[95] "Figura coeli hora institutionis universitatis Histropolitanae": Wien Nationalbibl. 24. fol. 212 verso; L. Thorndike, *A History of Magic and Experimental Science*, Vol. IV (History of Science Society Publications, New Series IV), New York, Columbia University Press, 1934, 1966, p. 420; [For the description of the manuscript:] F. Unterkircher, *Inventar der illuminierten Handschriften, Inkunabeln und Frühdrucke der Österreichischen Nationalbibliothek* (Museion, Veröffentlichungen der Österreichischen Nationalbibliothek), Teil I: *Die abendländischen Handschriften*, Wien, 1957, p. 24 (Plate no. 9).

[96] L. Hain, *Repertorium Bibliographicum*, no. 13801; F. R. Goff, *Incunabula in American Libraries*, New York, 1964, Third Census. R. 112 (R 107) (Plate no. 10).

[97] "Quemquidem librum Tabularum composuit dnus mgr. Joannes de Künigsberg [on the margin 'de Regiomonte'] in arce Strigoniensi a. d. 1467. cui composicioni predictus mgr. Martinus aderat et in pluribus audiutorio fuit etc." (Cracow, University Library, Ms. 597, III. 59); J. Csontosi, "A Krakkói

Könyvtár hazai vonatkozású kéziratai" [Manuscripts of the University Library of Cracow with material on History of Hungary], *Magyar Könyvszemle*, 1882, p. 385.

[98] "So haben meine herrn gert *die toktores*, die her sein chomen, am mantag vor Marie Madalene im 67 Jar, umb die hochschuell anzuheben, mit huener und mit semeln und mit wein, macht 10 s 8 d, und mit vischen 6 s 13 d, und mit pieren und marillen und czittber und mit plutzern umb 77 d; facit totum 2 L 3 s 22 d"; M. Császár, *Academia Istropolitana*, p. 106 document no. 6. cf. Ábel, *Egyetemeink a középkorban* [Hungarian Universities in the Middle Ages], p. 69, note 38.

[99] München, CLM. 18782, fol. 208 recto-215 recto; Strasbourg, 111, fol. 17 recto-27 verso; Thorndike, *A History of Magic and Experimental Science*, New York and London, 1966, Vol. IV, pp. 419–421.

[100] Wien, University Archives, *Acta Fac. Artium*, Lib. III, fol. 317 verso reported by L. S. Domonkos, *A History of Three Early Universities: Óbuda, Pozsony and Buda. Dissertation*, The Mediaeval Institute, Notre Dame, Indiana, 1966 (In typescript), p. 104; Cf. also, L. Némethy, *Series parochiarum archi-diocesis Strigoniensis*, Strigonii, 1894, II, p. 641.

[101] L. Juhász, ed, *Galeottus Martius Narniensis, De egregie, sapienter, iocose dictis ac factis Regis Mathiae ad ducem Iohannem eius filium liber* (Bibliotheca Scriptorum Medii Recentisque Aevorum. Saeculum XV), Lipsiae, 1934, pp. 30–33.

[102] "Qui et duos libros Sententiarum in Histropoli legit": M. Császár, *Academia Istropolitana*, p. 117, no. 17; Ábel, *Egyetemeink a középkorban* [Hungarian Universities in the Middle Ages], p. 72.

Laurencius Coci de Krumpach matriculated into the Hungarian Nation at the University of Vienna as *pauper* on April 14, 1449. See K. Schrauf, *Magyarországi tanulók a bécsi Egyetemen* [Hungarian Students at the University of Vienna], Budapest, 1892, p. 107; F. Gall, *Die Matrikel der Universität Wien*, 1377–1450, p. 269.

[103] "Rogamus vos, et cum eo, – videlicet Magistro prememorato – dispensare velitis et lectiones per eum legi debendas simul et alios actus quos ex statuto vestro perficere habet in Universitate Istropolitana continuari permittatis": Császár, *ibid.*, pp. 115–116, document 15; Ábel, *ibid.*, p. 72, note 43.

[104] [1470, nov. 23] "Exauditus fuit absolute magister Stephanus Murer de Brunn, qui petivit concedi magistro Nicolao de Hittendorf in theologia licentiato, tunc in nova universitate Histropolensi, videlicet Posoniensi lectori, quendam librum pro exemplari de libraria facultatis": Wien, University Archives, *Acta Fac. Art.* III, fol. 211 recto; Császár, *ibid.*, p. 116, document 16; Ábel, *ibid.*, p. 73, note 44.

[105] In a deed of 1470 referring to the Olgyai Chege family, several clerics – Benedictus Polýan, Ludovicus de Pákos, Johannes de Szenthmihály, and Johannes Zenthgergh [Szentgyörgy] – were mentioned as *studentes in eadem alma Universitate hijstropolitana* (Budapest *National Archives* DL 88497, Plate no. 15). Franciscus Ethey, pastor of Kéthely and public notary in *universitate Ystropolitana* (DL 88501), and Paul, Archdeacon of Mosony, both *nunc in universitate Posoniensi constituti*, were also subjects of the University (Budapest *National Archives* DL 88502). The Dean of the Faculty of Arts at that time was Johannes de Cracovia. Also present at the University of Pozsony was Johannes de Kuppferberth, Master of Arts (Budapest *National Archives* DL 88505).

[106] "Sed illis credite, qui in Universitate Histropolitana viderunt operam meam, qualis fuit erga filium vestrum": G. Schönherr, "Középkori iskolázásunk történetéhez" [Contribution to the History of Mediaeval Education in Hungary], *Magyar Könyvszemle*, (1890) p.17. See also note 105.

[107] W. Szaivert – F. Gall, *Die Matrikel der Universität Wien 1451–1518/I Text* (Publikationen des Instituts für Österreichische Geschichtsforschung VI. Reihe), Graz-Wien-Köln, 1967, II, Band, 128; 137; 139.

[108] *Ibid.*, 122; 127; 134; 137; 139; 141.

[109] "Academia amplissima in Posidonia idest possoni": Ábel, *Egyetemeink a középkorban* [Hungarian Universities in the Middle Ages], p. 79, note 52.

[110] Ábel, *ibid.*, p. 37, note 64; cf. Császár, *Academia Istropolitana*, p. 128, document 32.

[111] T. Pauler, *A budapesti magyar kir. Tudomány-Egyetem története* [History of the University of Budapest], Budapest, 1880, I, 120; 122; Szentpétery, *A Bölcsészettudományi Kar története 1634–1935* [History of the Faculty of Philosophy of the University of Budapest], Budapest, 1935 (A királyi magyar

Pázmány Péter-Tudományegyetem története IV), Budapest, 1935, 3–4.

[112] G. Prévot, "La haute note jaune", *Nouvelle Revue Française* [30] 1967 [September], p. 475.

* I would like to express my appreciation and gratitude to my dear friend, Mr. Wallace V. Bedolfe, President, United Casualty Agencies Limited, Toronto, for his continued interest and encouragement in my research and publications.

BIBLIOGRAPHY

Ábel, J., *Egyetemeink a középkorban* [Hungarian Universities in the Middle Ages], Budapest, 1881.

Alain, *Propos sur le bonheur*, Paris, Gallimard, 1928.

Album seu Matricula Facultatis Juridicae Universitatis Pragensis, ab anno Christi 1372. usque ad annum 1418, Pars I (Monumenta historica Universitatis Carolo-Ferdinandeae Pragensis, Tomus II), Prague, 1834.

Ashbach, J., *Geschichte der Wiener Universität im ersten Jahrhunderte ihres Bestehen. Festschrift zu ihrer fünfhundertjährigen Gründungsfeier*, Wien, 1865.

Bako, E., – Horváth, M. J., *Six Hundred Years of Hungarian University Education. Catalog*, College Park, Maryland, 1967.

Ballus von, P., *Presburg und seine Umgebungen*, Presburg, 1823.

Balogh, J., *A művészet Mátyás király udvarában* [Art in the Court of Matthias Corvinus], Budapest, 1966, vols. I and II.

Barna, Nándor, *Jellemvonások Mátyás király életéböl, a szemtanú Galeotti Latin Müve után* [Matthias Corvinus According to Galeotti], Pest, 1862.

Békefi, R., *A Pécsi Egyetem* [University of Pécs], Budapest, 1909.

Belnay, G. A., *Historia Literarum Bonarumque artium in Hungaria e probatissimis Scriptoribus synoptice deducta*, Viennae – Posonii – Cassoviae – Pestini, 1799.

Bergel, J., Blaschka, A., und Schreiber, R., *Studien zur Geschichte der Karls-Universität zu Prag*, Salzburg, 1954.

Bónis, G., "Einflüsse des römischen Rechts in Ungarn", *Ius Romanum Medii Aevi*, Pars V, 10, Milano, 1964 [1–113].

65

Bónis, G., "Magyi János formuláskönyve és a gyakorlati jogtanítás" [Le formulaire de János Magyi et l'enseignement pratique du Droit], Csizmadia, A., ed., *A pécsi Egyetem történetéből* [From the History of the University of Pécs] (Jubileumi Tanulmánok), Pécs, 1967, 225–260.

Borovszky, S., ed., *Pozsony vármegye (Magyarország vármegyéi és városai)* [Comitat of Pozsony Bratislava], Budapest, s. d.

Bullae Bonifacii IX. P. M. Pars altera, 1396–1404. (Monumenta Vaticana historiam Regni Hungariae illustrantia), Budapest, 1889. Series I. Tomus IV.

Codex Diplomaticus Universitatis Studii Generalis Cracoviensis, Pars Prima = 1365–1440 =, Cracow, 1870.

Colle, F. M., *Storia Scientifico-letteraria dello Studio di Padova*, 4 vols., Padova, 1824–1825, Vol. II.

Császár, M., *Az Academia Istropolitana, Mátyás király pozsonyi Egyeteme* [Academia Istropolitana, University of Matthias Corvinus at Pozsony], Pozsonyi, 1914.

Csizmadia, A., ed., *A pécsi Egyetem történetéből* [From the History of the University of Pécs] (Jubileumi Tanulmányok), Pécs, 1967.

Csizmadia, A., "Galvano di Bologna pécsi működése és a középkori magyar jogi oktatás egyes kérdései" [The Activities of Galvanus of Bologna and Some Problems in the Teaching of Law in Medieval Hungary], Csizmadia, A., ed., *A pécsi Egyetem történetéből* [From the History of the University of Pécs] (Jubileumi Tanumányok), Pécs, 1967, 111–128.

Csizmadia, A., *L'Université de Pécs au moyen âge.* (1367.) (Studia Iuridica auctoritate Universitatis Pécs publicata no. 42), Budapest, 1965.

Csontosi, J., "A krakkói Könyvtár hazai vonatkozású kéziratai" [Manuscripts of the University Library of Cracow with Material on History of Hungary], *Magyar Könyvszemle*, 1882, 373–398.

Davy, M., *Les sermons universitaires Parisiens de 1250–1251. Contribution à l'histoire de la prédication médiévale* (Etudes de Philosophie Médiévale no. 15), Paris, 1931.

Denifle, H., – Chatelain, Ae., ed., *Chartularium Universitatis Parisiensis*, I–IV, Paris, 1889–1897.

Denis, M., *Codices manuscripti theologici Bibliothecae Palatinae Vindobonensis Latini*, Vol. I Pars III, Vindobonae, 1795.

Dercsényi, D., *Nagy Lajos kora* [The Century of Louis the Great, King of Hungary], Budapest, s. d.

Dercsényi, D., – Pogány, F., – Szentkirályi, Z., *Pécs* [The City of Pécs] (Városképek-Műemlékek), Budapest, 1956.

Domanovszky, A., "Chronici Hungarici Compositio Saeculi XIV", Szentpétery, E., ed., *Scriptores rerum hungaricarum*, 1937, I, pp. 217–505.

Domonkos, L. S., *A History of Three Early Hungarian Universities: Óbuda, Pozsony, and Buda. Dissertation*. The Mediaeval Institute, Notre Dame, Indiana, 1966 (In typescript).

Domonkos, L. S., "The History of the Sigismundean Foundation of the University of Óbuda (Hungary)", *Studium Generale, Studies Offered to Astrik L. Gabriel* (Texts and Studies in the History of Mediaeval Education, No. XI), Notre Dame, Indiana, 1967, 3–33.

Erler, G., *Die Matrikel der Universität Leipzig, Die Immatrikulationen von 1409–1559*, Leipzig, Giesecke and Devrient, 1895.

Fraknói, V., *Magyarország egyházi és politikai összeköttetései a Római Szentszékkel* [Ecclesiastical and Political Rapports between Hungary and the Holy See], Budapest, 1901.

Fraknói, V., *Mátyás Király Levelei* [The Correspondence of Matthias Corvinus], Budapest, 1893, vol. I, 1458–1479; vol. II, 1480–1490.

Frank, I. W., O. P., "Leonhard Huntpichler O. P. († 1478) Theologieprofessor und Ordensreformer in Wien", *Archivum Fratrum Praedicatorum*, 36 (1966) 313–388.

Gabriel, A. L., *Les rapports dynastiques franco-hongrois au moyen-âge*, Budapest, 1944.

Gabriel, A. L., *Magyar diákok és tanárok a középkori Párizsban* [La vie à Paris des étudiants hongrois au moyen âge], Budapest, 1938.

Gál, I. *Ungarische Städtebilder*, Budapest, n. d.

Gall, F., *Alma Mater Rudolphina 1365–1965, Die Wiener Universität und Ihre Studenten*, Wien, 1965.

[Gall, F.], *Die Matrikel der Universität Wien, 1377–1450* (Publikationen des Instituts für Österreichische Geschichtsforschung), Graz-Köln, 1956, I. Band.

Gall, F., "Gründung und Anfänge der Wiener Universität", *Les universités européennes du XIVe au XVIIIe siècle. Aspects et Problèmes* (Institut d'Histoire de la Faculté des Lettres de l'Université de Genève no. 4), Genève, 1967.

Gereczi, P., A pécsi régi egyetem helye és cimere" [The Location and Arms of the Old University of Pécs], *Archaeologiai Értesitö*, (1904) 193–195.

Gewirth, A., *Marsilius of Padua, The Defender of Peace*, New York, 1951, 1956, 2 vols.

Goff, F. R., *Incunabula in American Libraries*, Third Census, New York, 1964.

Grundman, H. "Sacerdotium, Regnum, Studium", *Archiv für Kulturgeschichte*, 34 (1951) 5–21.

Hain, L., *Repertorium Bibliographicum*, Berlin, 1925, 2 vols.

Heilig, K., "Zur Geschichte der ältesten Ungarischen Universitäten und des Magisters Benedikt von Makra", *Jahrbuch des Wiener ungarischen Historischen Instituts*, I (1431), 41–49.

Horváth, J., *Az Irodalmi Müveltség Megoszlása* [History of Hungarian Literature in the Renaissance Period], Budapest, 1944.

Istvánffy, N. [M], *Regni hungarici Historia, per Nicolaum Isthuanffium Pannonium ejusdem Regni Propalatinum, libris XXXIV. exacte descripta*, Cologne, 1685.

Juhász, L., ed., *Galeottus Martius Narniensis, De egregie, sapienter, iocose dictis ac factis Regis Mathiae ad ducem Iohannem eius filium liber* (Bibliotheca Scriptorum Medii Recentisque Aevorum. Saeculum XV), Lipsiae, 1934.

Kálti, M., *Die ungarische Bilderchronik, Chronica de Gestis Hungarorum*, Berlin, Rütten and Loening, 1961.

Karácsonyi, J., *Szt. Ferencz Rendjének történeteMagyarországon 1711-ig* [The History of the Franciscan Order in Hungary till 1711], Budapest, 1922–1924, 2 vols.

Kavka, F., "A prágai Károly egyetem, a pécsi egyetem és Dél-Magyarország a XIV. században és a XV. század elején

[The University of Charles of Prague, the University of Pécs, and Southern Hungary in the XIVth and the Beginning of the XVth Centuries], Csizmadia, A., ed., *A pécsi Egyetem történetéből* [From the History of the University of Pécs] (Jubileumi Tanumányok), Pécs, 1967, 87–95.

Kazy, F., *Historia Universitatis Tyrnaviensis Societatis Jesu*, Tyrnaviae, 1738.

Kleineidam, E., *Universitas Studii Erffordensis*. Teil I: 1392–1460, Leipzig, 1964.

Koller, J., *Historia episcopatus Quinqueecclesiarum*, Tomus III, Tomus IV, Posonii, 1784, 1796.

Kosáry, D. G., *A History of Hungary*, Cleveland, 1941.

Kozlowska-Budkowa, S., – Kavka, F., – Kovács, E., – Gall, F., – Stelling-Michaud, S., – Garin, E., – Le Goff, J., – Pantin, W. A., – Steinmetz, M., – Lesnodorski, B., – Novicky, G. A., *Les universités européennes du XIVe au XVIIIe siècle. Aspects et Problèmes* (Institut d'Histoire de la Faculté des Lettres de Genève no. 4), Genève, 1967.

Lagarde, G. de, *La naissance de l'esprit laïque au déclin du Moyen Age*, II, *Marsile de Padoue ou le premier théoricien de l'état laïque*, Paris, 1948.

Lang, J., *Die Christologie bei Heinrich von Langenstein*, Freiburg, Basel, Wien, 1966.

Liber decanorum Facultatis Philosophicae Universitatis Pragensis, ab anno Christi 1367 usque ad annum 1585, Pars I (Monumenta historica Universitatis Carolo-Ferdinandeae Pragensis, Tome I), Prague, 1830. [Abbreviated Mon. Univ. Prag.).

Lukinich, L., ed., *Mátyás király. Emlékkönyv születésének ötszázéves fordulójára* [Mélanges in Memory of the Five-Hundredth Year Anniversary of the Birth of Matthias Corvinus, King of Hungary], Budapest, s. d. I–88. v.

Némethy, L., *Series parochiarum et parochorum archi-diocesis Strigoniensis*, Strigonii, 1894, I–II vols.

Oláh, N. [M.], *Nicolai Olahi metropolitae Strigoniensis Hungaria et Atila sive de originibus gentis, regni Hungariae situ, habitu, opportunitatibus et rebus bello paceque ab Atila gestis libri duo*, Vindobonae, 1763.

69

Pauler, T., *A budapesti magyar kir. Tudomány-Egyetem története* [History of the University of Budapest], Budapest, 1880, I.

Petrovich, E., "A középkori pécsi Egyetem megszűnése [Wie lange bestand die mittelalterliche Universität in Pécs?], *Janus Pannonius Múzeum*, 1966, 153–170.

Petrovich, E., "A pécsi egyetemi beszédgyűjtemény" [A Collection of Sermons Given at the University of Pécs], Csizmadia, A., ed., *A pécsi egyetem történetéből* [From the History of the University of Pécs] (Jubileumi Tanulmányok), Pécs, 1967, 163–223.

[Ulrich von Richental] *Das Concilium So zu Constanz gehalten ist worden*, Heinrich Stainer, ed. (Augsburg, 1536). *Ulrich von Richental "Chronik des Constanzer Concils 1414 bis 1418"*, Text der Aulendorfer Handschrift, Unveränderter Neudruck der von Richard Michael Buck besorgten Ausgabe, 1936 (F. W. Hendel Verlag zu Meersburg am Bodensee und Leipzig), fol. CXXIIII verso.

Ritter, G., *Studien zur Spätscholastik* (Sitzungsberichte der Heidelberger Akademie der Wissenschaften, Philosophisch-historische Klasse, 1922, Abhandlung 7), II: *Via antiqua und via moderna auf den deutschen Universitäten des XV. Jahrhunderts*, Heidelberg, 1922.

Schönherr, G., "Középkori iskolázásunk történetéhez" (Contribution to the History of Mediaeval Education in Hungary], *Magyar Könyvszemle*, 1890, 11–20.

Schrauf, K., *Magyarországi tanulók a bécsi egyetemen* [Hungarian Students at the University of Vienna] (Magyarországi tanulók külföldön II), Budapest, 1892.

Schulte von, J. F., *Die Geschichte der Quellen und Literatur des Canonischen Rechts von der Mitte des 16. Jahrhunderts bis zur Gegenwart* (Die Geschichte der Quellen und Literatur des Canonischen Rechts von Gratian bis auf die Gegenwart), III, Stuttgart, 1880.

Seton-Watson, R. W., *Prague Essays Presented by a Group of British Historians to the Caroline University of Prague on the Occasion of Its Six-Hundredth Anniversary*, Oxford, 1949.

70

Simonyi, D., "Pécs 'Quinque Ecclesiae' nevének eredetéről" [The Origin of the Name of Pécs 'Quinque Ecclesiae'], *Antik Tanulmányok. Studia Antiqua*, 6 (1959) 87–103.

Stručné Dějiny University Karlovy, Praha, 1964.

Szabó, P. Z., "Der Mittelpunkt Südpannoniens", Gál, I., ed. *Ungarische Städtebilder*, Budapest, s. d., 147–157.

Szaivert, W., – Gall, F., *Die Matrikel der Universität Wien 1451–1518/I Text* (Publikationen des Instituts für Österreichische Geschichtsforschung, VI. Reihe), Graz-Wien-Köln, 1967, II. Band.

Szathmáry, L., "Az asztrológia, alkémia és misztika Mátyás király udvarában" [Astrology, Alchemy and Mysticism in the Court of Matthias Corvinus], *Mátyás Király Emlékkönyv*, II, 413–452, Budapest, s. d.

Szentpétery, I., *A Bölcsészettudományi Kar története 1634–1935* [History of the Faculty of Philosophy of the University of Budapest], Budapest, 1935 (A királyi magyar Pázmány Péter-Tudományegyetem története IV), Budapest, 1935.

Szentpétery, I., ed., *Scriptores rerum hungaricarum*, I–II, Budapest, 1937–1938.

Theiner (ed.), *Bullae Bonifacii IX. P. M. IX Bonifácz Pápa Bullái 1389–1396* (Monumenta Vaticana historiam regni Hungariae illustrantia. Series prima, Tomus III), Budapestini, 1888.

Theiner, A., *Vetera monumenta historiae Hungariae sacrae illustrata*, 2 vols., Rome, 1860.

Thorndike, L., *A History of Magic and Experimental Science*, Vol. IV (History of Science Society Publications, New Series IV), New York, Columbia University Press, 1934, 1966.

Unterkircher, F., *Inventar der illuminierten Handschriften, Inkunabeln und Frühdrucke der Österreichischen Nationalbibliothek* (Museion, Veröffentlichungen der Österreichischen Nationalbibliothek), Teil I: *Die abendländischen Handschriften*, Wien, 1957.

Várady, E., *Docenti e scolari ungheresi nell'antico Studio Bolognese*, Bologna, 1951.

Veress, A., *Matricula et Acta Hungarorum in Universitatibus Italiae Studentium 1221–1864* (Monumenta Hungariae Italica no. 3), Budapestini, 1941.

71

Vetulani, A., "A pécsi egyetem, valamint a krakkói és bécsi testvéregyetemek alapításának körülményei" [Les circonstances accompagnant la fondation de l'Université de Pécs et ses universités-soeurs de Cracovie et de Vienne], Csizmadia, A., ed., *A Pécsi Egyetem Történetéből* [From the History of the University of Pécs], Pécs, 1967, pp. 21–51.

LIST OF ILLUSTRATIONS PLATES

Plate. no. 1. (Vatican Archives, Reg. Vat. no. 256, fol. 68 verso.) Viterbo, 1367, September 2. Pope Urban V informs Louis the Great, King of Hungary, of the approval of the University of Pécs: *Carissimo in Christo filio Ludovico Regi Ungarie illustri salutem [et apostolicam benedictionem]. Decet regiam celsitudinem . . .* Below: *Ad perpetuam rei memoriam in supreme dignitatis apostolice specula. . .* dated Viterbo, 1367, September 1, Pope Urban V approves the foundation of the University of Pécs

Plate no. 2. (Vatican Archives, Reg. Avenion. n. 164, fol. 502 recto; olim Urban V. An. V. Par. I-a, Tome XV. fol. 502 recto.) Viterbo, 1367, September 12. Pope Urban V, at the request of Louis the Great, King of Hungary (1342—1382), grants dispensation to the doctors, masters, and students of the University of Pécs from the obligation of residence: *Dilectis filiis, universis doctoribus, magistris et scolaribus studii Quinqueecclesiensis . . .*

Plate no. 3. (Vatican Archives, Reg. Vat. 285, fol. 115 recto; olim Greg. XI., De ind. et privileg. An IV. fol. 115 recto.) Villeneuve dioc., Avignon. 1374, August 3. Pope Gregory XI instructs the University of Bologna to receive Galvanus de Bologna, a former master at the University of Pécs, into their society: *Dilectis filiis . . . rectoribus, doctoribus, Collegio et Universitati studii iuris canonici . . .*

Plate no. 4. (Vatican Archives, Reg. Avenion. no. 170, fol. 541 recto; olim Urban V. An. VII. Par. II. Tom. 21. fol. 541 recto.) Rome, 1369, April 2. Pope Urban V orders Cato, provost of Bács in Hungary, to confer the doctorate in Canon Law at the University of Pécs upon Paul, provost of Szeben, if he proves himself deserving: *Dilecto filio Catoni, preposito Baciensi salutem etc. Cum, sicut accepimus* . . .

Plate no. 5. (München, Bayerische Staatsbibliothek, CLM 22363 fol. 179 recto [67r]) MS. early fifteenth century. Facsimile of the beginning of a sermon on Saint Stephen, King of Hungary, composed at the University of Pécs

Plate no. 6. (Vatican Archives, Reg. Suppl. 581, fol. 55 verso; olim Paul II. vol. 810, fol. 55 verso.) Rome, 1465, May 19. Matthias Corvinus, King of Hungary, asks Pope Paul II to found a university in Hungary on the model of that of Bologna: *Beatissime Pater. In regno Ungarie licet amplo et fertili, non viget aliquod studium generale* . . .

Plate no. 7. (The New York Public Library. Spencer Collection, Ms. 32, p. 417.) Arms of the University of Buda (above) and Bologna (below)

Plate no. 8. View of Pozsony (Pressburg, Bratislava), in Johann Christoph Wagner's *Delineatio Pannoniae*, Augsburg, 1685

Plate no. 9. (Wien, Österreichische Nationalbibliothek, Cod. 24, fol. 212 verso.) Horoscope of the University of Pozsony, composed by Martinus Ilkusch in 1467 and copied into Ptolemaeus, *Almagest*, executed around 1489 in Buda

Plate no. 10. Dedication of Johannes Regiomontanus, *Tabulae directionum et profectionum* (ed. Johannes Angelus), Augsburg, Erhard Ratdolt, 2. Jan. 1490, to Johannes Vitéz, archbishop of Esztergom. (Brandeis University Library copy. cf. F. R. Goff, *Incunabula in American Libraries*, New York, 1964, p. 523, no. R.-112)

Plate no. 11. (New York City, The Pierpont Morgan Library, Ms. 496, fol. 2 recto.) Portrait of Matthias Corvinus, King of Hungary. A full-page miniature from Saint Didymus Alexandrinus, *De Spiritu Sancto*, representing Saint Jerome in medallion and Matthias Corvinus kneeling, looking in admiration at the Saint. Cf. J. Balogh, "Mátyás kiraly arcképei" [Portraits of Matthias Corvinus], *Mátyás Király Emlékkönyv*, Budapest, s. d., p. 503, no. 40

Plate no. 12. (New York City, The Pierpont Morgan Library, Ms. 496, fol. 2 recto.) Portrait of Matthias Corvinus, King of Hungary. Detail of a larger, full-page miniature executed by the brothers Gherardo and Monte del Fora in 1488. Cf. J. Balogh, "Mátyás király arcképei [Portraits of Matthias Corvinus], *Mátyás Király Emlékkönyv*, Budapest, s. d., I, p. 503, no. 40

Plate no. 13. (Heidelberg, Universitätsbibliothek, Cod. Pal germ. 156, fol. 164 recto.) Portrait of Matthias Corvinus King of Hungary, executed by a German artist circa 1495 The German translation of the Chronicle of John Thuróczy Cf. J. Balogh, "Mátyás király arcképei" [Portraits of Matthias Corvinus], *Mátyás Király Emlékkönyv*, Budapest, s. d., p. 508. no. 47

Plate no. 14. (Vatican Library, Ms. Rossian. no. 1164, fol. 126 verso.) Matthias Corvinus, King of Hungary, kneeling before the *Vir Dolorum*. Executed around 1469. Cf. J. Balogh, "Mátyás király arcképei" [Portraits of Matthias Corvinus], *Mátyás Király Emlékkönyv*, Budapest, s. d., p. 504, no. 41

Plate no. 15. (Budapest, National Archives [Országos Levéltár] DL 88497.) A deed of 1470 April 2, referring to several subjects in *domo habitacionis Burse studentium* of the University of Pozsony in *eadem alma Universitate hÿstropolitana*

Plate no. 16. Map of Hungary with the sites of the University of Pécs (*5 Kirchen*), Pozsony (*Pressburg*), and Buda (*Ofen*), in Johann Christoph Wagner's *Delineatio Pannoniae*, Augsburg, 1685

Plate no. 17. View of Buda (at right) with the city of Pest (left) in Johann Christoph Wagner's *Delineatio Pannoniae*, Augsburg, 1685

INDEX

MANUSCRIPTS AND ARCHIVES MATERIAL

Budapest, *National Archives, DL 88497* [See p. 63, plate no. 15]
Budapest, *National Archives, DL 88501* [63]
Budapest, *National Archives, DL 88502* [63]
Budapest, *National Archives, DL 88505* [63]
Cracow, *University Library, Ms. 597, III, 59* [61]
Heidelberg, *Universitätsbibliothek, Cod. Pal. germ. 156, fol. 164r* [75, plate no. 13]
München, *Bayerische Staatsbibliothek, CLM 18782, fol. 208r–215r* [62]
München, *Bayerische Staatsbibliothek, CLM 22363, fol. 67r, 68r, 69v* [57, 74, plate no. 5]
New York Public Library, Spencer collection, *Ms. 32, p. 417* [74, plate no. 7]
New York Pierpont Morgan Library, *Ms. 496, fol. 2r* [74, 75, plates nos. 11, 12]
Strasbourg, Bibl. Universitaire, *Ms. 111, fol. 17r–27v* [62]
Vatican Archives, *Reg. Avenion. no. 164, fol. 502r* [73, plate no. 2]
Vatican Archives, *Reg. Suppl. 581, fol. 55v–56r* [58, 74, plate no. 6]
Vatican Archives, *Reg. Vat. 256, fol. 68v* [73, plate no. 1]
Vatican Archives, *Reg. Vat. 285, fol. 115r* [73, plate no. 3]
Vatican Library, *Cod. Ottobon. Lat. no. 689, fol. 131r–142r* [60]
Vatican Library, *Ms. Rossian., no. 1164, fol. 126v* [75, plate no. 14]
Vatican Library, *Vat. Lat. 2660, fol. 100v–106v* [54]
Vatican Library, *Vat. Lat. 2683, fol. 225r–227r* [54]
Wien, Österreichische Nationalbibliothek, *Cod. 24, fol. 212v* [74, plate no. 9]
Wien, University Archives, *Acta Facultatis Artium, Lib. III, fol. 211r–317v* [62, 63]

ILLUSTRATIONS

PLATES

Plate no. 1. (Vatican Archives, Reg. Vat. no. 256, fol. 68 verso.) Viterbo, 1367, September 2. Pope Urban V informs Louis the Great, King of Hungary, of the approval of the University of Pécs: *Carissimo in Christo filio Ludovico Regi Ungarie illustri salutem [et apostolicam benedictionem]. Decet regiam celsitudinem* ... Below: *Ad perpetuam rei memoriam in supreme dignitatis apostolice specula* ... dated Viterbo, 1367, September 1, Pope Urban V approves the foundation of the University of Pécs

Plate no. 2. (Vatican Archives, Reg. Avenion. n. 164, fol. 502 recto; olim Urban V. An. V. Par. I–a, Tome XV. fol. 502 recto.) Viterbo, 1367, September 12. Pope Urban V, at the request of Louis the Great, King of Hungary (1342–1382), grants dispensation to the doctors, masters, and students of the University of Pécs from the obligation of residence: *Dilectis filiis, universis doctoribus, magistris et scolaribus studii Quinqueecclesiensis* . . .

Plate no. 3 (Vatican Archives, Reg. Vat. 285, fol. 115 recto; olim Greg. XI., De ind. et privileg. An IV. fol. 115 recto.) Villeneuve dioc., Avignon. 1374, August 3. Pope Gregory XI instructs the University of Bologna to receive Galvanus de Bologna, a former master at the University of Pécs, into their society: *Dilectis filiis . . . rectoribus, doctoribus, Collegio et Universitati studii iuris canonici . . .*

Plate no. 4. (Vatican Archives, Reg. Avenion. no. 170, fol. 541 recto; olim Urban V. An. VII. Par. II. Tom. 21. fol. 541 recto.) Rome, 1369, April 2. Pope Urban V orders Cato, provost of Bács in Hungary, to confer the doctorate in Canon Law at the University of Pécs upon Paul, provost of Szeben, if he proves himself deserving: *Dilecto filio Catoni, preposito Baciensi salutem etc. Cum, sicut accepimus . . .*

Dilecto filio Catoni p̄poſito Baien. Saluté &c. Cum sicut accepimus dilecti filii Pauli
p̄poſiti Colinien. adeo in iure canonico facultate sufficienti p̄ſeruit in eaq̄ quam
ea p̄itus exiſtit et digne meret in ipſa facultate honore &c. inſignia ver3 doctoribus
sint nobis p̄ipris Pauli parte ſuali ſupplicatū ut ipm ad honorē dñi doctoratus
munire de benignitate apta dignaremini Nos itaq̄ huius ſupplicib3 inclinati diſcrecioni
tue &c. ipſa in dño fiduciam gerentes ṕales eidem Paulo in ciuitate Cumqueeccleñ
si ipm p̄ diligentis examinacionem adſoz ydoneū et ſufficienté eſſe reperis doctoratus honoré
et docendi licenciam ſuali ſolemnitatib3 in talib3 ġſueti queſt appēa ṗcedendi No obſtan
quibuſcūq̄ priuilegijs ac ſtatutis et ġſuetudi ſtudij Cumqueeccleñ et alioz quozcūq̄ ſtudioz
ġt ipis unḡoſit eſmaioz apta ut quatinus ciuitate illa roboratis eſſe de illis et conſue
toz tenorib3 ṕalis et expreſſa ac de verbo ad verbū eſſet in publis metro facienda que
alias noluimus in ſuo robore ṕmaner plena et liberam oꝛdinemus tenore ṕium facultatem
Dat. Rome apud Sanctpetr. III Non. Aprilis Anno Septimo

Venli fri Johanni epo Iſten. Saluté &c. Sincere deuocionis affectus quē ad nos et Romani geñt
ecclam te indigne merere ut peticionib3 tuis illis p̄ſtd p̄ quas anime tue conſulatur
ſalus fauorabilr Annuimus Hinc est ġ nos tuis ſupplis inclinati tibi ut aliquē ydoneum
pbrm in diſcretum eligē habeas qui tecū hac vice diſpenſat ſup irregularitates materiā ſeq̄
p̄ deſenſone et tuitione iuriū tue p̄priy que in nonnullis caſtris et villis in diocesi et
eo deumq̄ obtinet epale forſitan incurriſti auctore iura diſpenſare tibiq̄ p̄oſſſe tua diligent
audita p̄ commiſſo etiā si talia ſuñt ipse que ſedes apta ſib iniūcto ġ penitē abſoluerenj
debeat impendere habeat ac penitencia iniunġe ſaluterim auctore apta de ṕali grā tenore ṕium
indulgemus Nullius ꝛc ius ġreſt infringē ꝛc Dat. apud monaſtſouium Non. Agui ponet
ur Anno Septimo

Dilecto filio Nobili viro Guidoni de Polenta militi Rauennas in Ciuitatibus Rauennat et
Ceruien. eozq̄ Comitatib3 et diſtrictibus necnon polente et Chuglanelli Caſtros ac villa
ayeſſe in ṕuincia Romandiole ad nos et Romani ecclam ṕtinentis conſtitutis p̄ nobis et ecclā ipſa
in ṕalibus vicario et Officiali Saluté &c. ꝓpte tue deuocionis et fidelitatis obſequia que nobis
et Romani eccle impendiſti liberalr hactinus et impendis no deſinis no indigne merete ut
iura liberaliter ġuari ꝓpeaq̄ṗ exhibita ſiquide nobis tue peticionis ſeries genuebat ġ tu q̄dam
Bernaduinus de Polenta ayles pater tuus et tu poſt eius obitu breuiatu gubernacem
adminiſtracem et regimē Ciuitatum Rauennat et Ceruien. ac eaz Comitatū et diſtrictuū
necnon Caſtroz polente et Chuglanelli et villa ayeſſe in ṕuincia Romandiole ad nos et Romani
ecclam ṕtinentis ġſtituentoz p̄ ſedē aptam ſeu eius auctore eidem tuo patri et tibi ġmiſſa ġcuſſuit
multis annis elaxſis vere ecle ṕlibate de benedſolue p̄ cenſu Annua eidē ecclē Triamilla
florenoz et duū floren auri ġ turn dict Ciuitat Ceruien. bony et legalis ponderis de florencia
in certis teminis ad hoc ſtatut tam dem tuus pater ſeu viuet qua tu poſt eius obitu in
aliquib3 ex teminis ṕdis p̄pt impoſſibilitate et nonnulla ineuitabilia cauſa expcāz cenſum
huiꝰ integre no ſoluiſſe p̄ ġ tu ratṅe penury et penuria et ṗſate Ciuitates Caſtra et
villa nubdſuas auctore apta ṕpdā ſi in huiꝰ ſolucꝰ cenſus defecis ṕmulgatas incurreſti

Plate no. 5. (München, Bayerische Staatsbibliothek, CLM 22363 fol. 179 recto [67r]) MS. early fifteenth century. Facsimile of the beginning of a sermon on Saint Stephen, King of Hungary, composed at the University of Pécs

Plate no. 6. (Vatican Archives, Reg. Suppl. 581, fol. 55 verso; olim Paul II. vol. 810, fol. 55 verso.) Rome, 1465, May 19. Matthias Corvinus, King of Hungary, asks Pope Paul II to found a university in Hungary on the model of that of Bologna: *Beatissime Pater. In regno Ungarie, licet amplo et fertili, non viget aliquod studium generale . . .*

... posse abeaud[us] offend[er] ... ... integrum

... ... Curicta sen ad eund[em] p[er]tinent[em]
supplic[atur] ... ... sibi gr[ati]a[m] facere ... dicto officiali ... in ...
... p[re]rogativa ... ... su[per]iorib[us] iud[ici] re-
mittere et mandare ... ... sibi p[er] p[re]dicta sup[er]
... ...
... ... iud[ic]i competente in sc[riptis]
... ...
... ... potestat[em]
... ... illeg[itim]e possessor[es]
... romana ... ...
... ... p[er] liberat[ion]e d[e]
... ... aut aliq[u]i aliis eg[..]
... Illa p[ro] remediis ... ... aut ...
... ... et ... ...
... ...
Et ex q[ua]nta ... publice offend[er]e ... ... aliquot
... ... lit[te]re p[er] ... ... et
pro expresso existat ... ...
at[que] p[ro]videat de eode[m] ... ... obstantib[us] ...
... Confess[i]o[n]e p[re]sentes ... ... i[n] pr[emis]sis
... ...

Ceteru[m] statui[m]us ... ...
... ... Confess[i]o[n]e ...
... ... obstant[e] ... ... p[re]latos ...
... habeant[ur] pro expresso

D[atum] Rome apud ... p[er] ... d[i]e decimo
... ... Anno p[rimo]

M[aster] ...

Plate no. 7. (The New York Public Library. Spencer Collection, Ms. 32, p. 417.) Arms of the University of Buda (above) and Bologna (below)

Dns p̄ Petrus tacwilfigr ┐
Willielmus Colober
Fita de Roland   Doctores Rector
Nels Pelsfigr
Martinus Cracouensis Danois ┘

Von der Schül zū dudensis In andern
die da coment mit dem Ertzbschof vo̊ Cran

Dns Hanrecy ptrus pridensis
Mattheus de Diernach   Doctores Intheologia
Thomas de Wissenburg
Tattheus de vico mercato
Nicolay bissnow   Doctores decretoy
Dns symon clostem Mgr In Medicine

¶ Von der Schül Bononij

Dns petrus Balonows ┐
Dns Iohes delidema   Doctores In Theologia
¶ Dns Raphahel de placencia ┘
Petrus Iacobi de Jauff   Licenciati In Iure Danois
Gregorius gwindin

Plate no. 8. View of Pozsony (Pressburg, Bratislava), in Johann Christoph Wagner's *Delineatio Pannoniae*, Augsburg, 1685

PRESBVRG.

1. Schloß da die Cron verwahret wird. 2. Stadtkirch. 3. Vorstatt. 4. Donaustrohm.

Plate no. 9. (Wien, Österreichische Nationalbibliothek, Cod. 24, fol. 212 verso.) Horoscope of the University of Pozsony, composed by Martinus Ilkusch in 1467 and copied into Ptolemaeus, *Almagest*, executed around 1489 in Buda

ed his etiam o̅ sure mihi expositis fermeq̅ omnibus
que ad hanc tantarum rerum considerationem
pertinent breuiter mea quidem sententia quan-
tum ad hodiernum usq̅ diem aut ad inueniendu
aut ad emendandum exquisitus et tempora con-
ferebant et docendi modus ad comoditatem specu-
lationis non ad ostentationem accomodatus petebat pertracta-
tis ydoneum hic modum ac finem. hec est compositio o̅secuta.

finis 17 Martij 1461

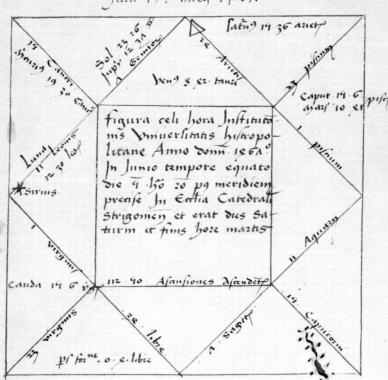

figura celi hora Institutionis Vniuersitatis hispo-
politane Anno domini 1461°
Jn Junio tempore equato
die 5 h̅o̅ 20 p̅ meridiem
precise Jn E̅c̅l̅ia Catedrali
Strigomen̅ et erat dies Sa-
turni et finis hore martis

Cuiu̅q̅ marius fuerit in duodecima erit magnus sapiens
magnus q̅ p̅hus   Messahala in antloquio.

Plate no. 10. Dedication of Johannes Regiomontanus, *Tabulae directionum et profectionum* (ed. Johannes Angelus), Augsburg, Erhard Ratdolt, 2. Jan. 1490, to Johannes Vitéz, archbishop of Esztergom. (Brandeis University Library copy. cf. F. R. Goff, *Incunabula in American Libraries*, New York, 1964, p. 523, no. R.-112)

Reuerendissimo in christo patri et dño: dño Joanni archiepo Strigonicn̄
legato rc. Joannes Bermanus de regiomonte se humiliter cōmendat.

Agnam esse admodū ⁊ fuisse semp̄ in edēdis
libris difficultatem mihi videri solet:dum re
uoluto maiorꝫ nostrorꝫ exemplaria:ac p̄sertim
eorū exordia conspicio: vbi pleriqꝫ tenuitatez
ingeniorꝫ suorum insimulant non suffecturaꝫ
videlicet cepto operi.Alij vero arduitate ten/
tati negocij pene deterreri videntur nonnulli
erratis suis veniam datum iri volunt dubiaꝫ
scribendi fortunaꝫ haud iniuria suspicantes.
Mihi aūt reuerendissime dñe:aliud preterea
accedit q̄ factu prorsus impossibile reor:assi
due sꝫ iussioni tue morem gerere ac demū iu
dicio tuo non minus acuito q̄ recto dignū ali
quid reddere.Tue pfecto monitioni nephas est cōtrauenire:qui enim licenti?
in me habeat imperium preter te mortalis nemo est.Tibi aūt lucubrationes
meas corāꝫ te tam rigido:q̄ p̄spicacissimo censore depromsero:labascet illico
ānus.Quis enim eruditissimus licet aliquid nouarum literarum impune tibi
afferet quippe qui omni doctrina ac virtute mirum in modū preditus es diui
narum humanarūqꝫ rerum plenam tenes cognitionem: omnibus cuiuscunqꝫ
literature cum te prebeas auditorez:omnes tn̄ excellentissima eruditione tua
antecellis adeo :vt discipulos sese fateanī quicunqꝫ in habitu preceptorꝫ ad te
accesserint.Quantus es q̄ profundus in sacris existas literꝫ:neminē ignorare
arbitror.Quid referā de iure pontificio:cuius noticia quidez ornamento tibi
est.Usus aūt dignitati tue pnecessarius quippe qui supra omnes platos regni
hungarie primatū tenes: vniuersa demū phia tibi familiaris est: discipline aūt
quadruuiales decus ⁊ gloriā pepererūt.Q̄ si ad negocia humana transeundi
detur licentia:quis non admirabitur imensam tuam prudentiam:ex qua toti?
regni hungarie gubernatio pendet.Ita tn̄ foris publica curas vt domi quoqꝫ
magnificentia tua ineffabilis demonstref in arce inquā strigoniensi ad cuius
restitutionez assiduam:etsi nullis parcas impensis:longe tn̄ ampliori sumptu
solertiorꝯ studio bibliothecas p̄ciosissimas ac omni genere codicū refertissi
mas instituisti. Quanta pterea ⁊ q̄ perhennē curam habeas condendi studij
generalis conclamatū esse iam pridem arbitror:cum ex vniuersis literatorum
cōsortijs oīm professionum doctissimos quosqꝫ viros accersere soleas: officio
fret? regij cancellarij supmi:cui cepto felicissimo:me quoqꝫ Wieñensis collegij
alumnū quantumcunqꝫ adesse voluisti:docturū videlicet quadruuiales facul/
tates.Uenienti igitur voluntatiꝫ tue morē gesturo mihi in primis id mādati
dedisti vt tabulas quasi dā directionū cōponerez que ⁊ vsu faciles ⁊ iudicibus

Plate no. 11. (New York City, The Pierpont Morgan Library, Ms. 496, fol. 2 recto.) Portrait of Matthias Corvinus, King of Hungary. A full-page miniature from Saint Didymus Alexandrinus, *De Spiritu Sancto*, representing Saint Jerome in medallion and Matthias Corvinus kneeling, looking in admiration at the Saint. Cf. J. Balogh, "Mátyás király arcképei" [Portraits of Matthias Corvinus], *Mátyás Király Emlékkönyv*, Budapest, s. d., p. 503, no. 40

INCIPIT PRAEFATIO S. HIERO
NYMI IN LIBRO S. DIDYMI
GRAECI MONACHI ALEXAN
DRINI DE SPIRITU SANCTO

Dum in babilone uersarer et pur
purate meretricis essem colonus et
iure quiritium uiuerem coloniali
quidi gartire de spiritu sancto et

Plate no. 12. (New York City, The Pierpont Morgan Library, Ms. 496, fol. 2 recto.) Portrait of Matthias Corvinus, King of Hungary. Detail of a larger, full-page miniature executed by the brothers Gherardo and Monte del Fora in 1488. Cf. J. Balogh, "Mátyás király arcképei [Portraits of Matthias Corvinus], *Mátyás Király Emlékkönyv*, Budapest, s. d., I, p. 503, no. 40

Plate no. 14. (Vatican Library, Ms. Rossian. no. 1164, fol. 126 verso.) Matthias Corvinus, King of Hungary, kneeling before the *Vir Dolorum*. Executed around 1469. Cf. J. Balogh, "Mátyás király arcképei" [Portraits of Matthias Corvinus], *Mátyás Király Emlékkönyv*, Budapest, s. d., p. 504 no. 41

THESVS·NAZA
REX·IVDEI

GO SMathias Rex hugarie cocessi hoc missale
fri Thome de hugaria p̃ cui° obini maneat pñs
liber in prouincia quã claudit diem extremum·

Plate no. 15. (Budapest, National Archives [Országos Levél-tár] DL 88497.) A deed of 1470 April 2, referring to several subjects in *domo habitacionis Burse studentium* of the University of Pozsony in *eadem alma Universitate hÿstropolitana*

Plate no. 16. Map of Hungary with the sites of the University of Pécs (*5 Kirchen*), Pozsony (*Pressburg*), and Buda (*Ofen*), in Johann Christoph Wagner's *Delineatio Pannoniae*, Augsburg, 1685

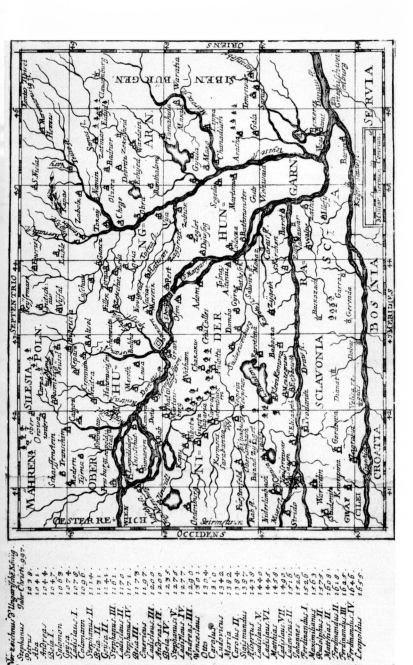

Plate no. 17. View of Buda (at right) with the city of Pest (left) in Johann Christoph Wagner's *Delineatio Pannoniae,* Augsburg, 1685

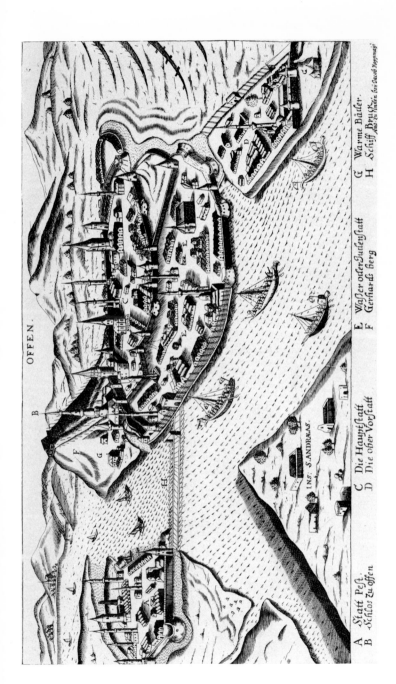

OFFEN.

INS. S.ANDREAS.

A Staff Peft.
B Schloß zu offen
C Die Hauptftatt
D Die ober Vorftatt
E Waßer oder Judenftatt
F Gerhard berg
G Warme Bäder.
H Schiff Bruck.

Aus zu finden bei Jacob Koppmayr